Greater

Things

ISBN Number: 978-1-7323972-0-0

Cover Design By: Andrea Hodges

Author Photo By: Aaron Jones

Connect With the Author:

Instagram: WriteTheWordMM

Twitter: WriteTheWordMM

https://inregardstolife.wordpress.com

This book is dedicated to you—the reader.

"I pray that the eyes of your heart may be enlightened in order that you may know the hope to which he has called you, the riches of his glorious inheritance in his holy people."

-Ephesians 1:18 (NIV)

Table of Contents

Introduction

"Very truly I tell you, whoever believes in me will do the works I have been doing, and they will do even greater things than these, because I am going to the Father." John 14:12 (NIV)

Who is Jesus, and what does it mean to be saved? The answers to these questions may vary from person to person, but every believer is called to the Great Commission, in which the world is reconciled to God through Jesus Christ. We are called to grow in the knowledge of God and spread the Gospel message to the ends of the Earth (Matthew 28:16-20). At times it seems that believers ask non-believers to follow Christ with hardly any knowledge of who He was on Earth, and who He is in heaven. Romans 10:14-15 (NLT) says,

"But how can they call on him to save them unless they believe in him? And how can they believe in him if they have never heard about him? And how can they hear about him unless someone tells them? And how will anyone go and tell them without being sent? That is why the Scriptures say, "How beautiful are the feet of messengers who bring good news!"

To have faith in Jesus, one must have an understanding of who He is, what it means to love, and be loved by Him. So, I ask again—who is Jesus? If you are a believer, how do you describe Him to someone who knows very little about Him? Do we leave this transfer of knowledge solely in the hands of pastors and evangelists? How do we define our own relationship with Christ? What we say about Jesus reveals a lot about ourselves, and that is true for believers and non-believers alike. This book is written in three phases that parallel 1 Corinthians 13:13 (NIV):

"And now these three remain: faith, hope and love. But the greatest of these is love."

If these things are what remain, or what is left in the end, are these not the greater things? Not cars, money, or status, but faith, hope, and love. This book is not intended to lay out guidelines for the reader to acquire worldly riches and possessions, but rather to achieve a greater understanding of the life of abundance God has called us to. These 'greater things' are not limited by this world, but span throughout eternity. Faith, hope, and love are the foundational principles that assist believers in their relationship with God. The difference between practicing a religion and establishing an intimate relationship with Christ is a religion gives a set of rules to follow to make you good enough, while Christianity depends on the goodness of Christ through His death to bring us into right standing with the Father. The only thing we can do to be 'good enough' for God is to believe in and accept His Son. It is only through His death that we are worthy of eternal life. Having a relationship with Jesus should greatly impact our actions, but we should not solely hold ourselves in high moral conduct because we are afraid of consequences, or think that our good works will get us into heaven. We operate in morality because we love Jesus and desire to look more like Him every day. The actions we display resonate louder than all of the words we could ever say.

Without faith, it is impossible to please God (Hebrews 11:6). If there is no faith then there is no evidence for our belief system. Faith gives us the ability to trust in God, who we will not always understand, but we acknowledge that He has our best interests at heart. Hope causes us to achieve what is insurmountable by holding on to what we believe, especially when it is not yet seen (2 Corinthians 4:16-18). Hope is the 'why' of our belief, and the expectation of receiving what we are asking God for. Lastly, love is the essence of who God is, because He is love (1 John 4:7-8). Love is the anchor for faith and hope, because He spans from everlasting to everlasting (Psalm 90:2). In the life of a Christian, all three elements must be established and strengthened to finish strong (2 Timothy

4:7-8). Now that you have read through these basic descriptions, ask yourself these questions:

- What am I hoping for?
- What am I expecting to happen in my life?
- Who is God to me?
- Do I believe that He has a plan for my life that is not limited by my thoughts?

It is my prayer, that whether you are growing in your faith, or desire a greater understanding of Christianity, that this book, under the guidance of the Holy Spirit, would lead you into Truth (John 8:31-32).

I once heard a preacher say that we should never place more emphasis on the messenger than the message. The messenger is not the message, and the messenger is never more important than the one who sent the message. Although books of this nature are meant to encourage and equip, our best line of defense in spiritual terms is the Word of God. The Bible is the compass of life, providing us with clarity, direction, comfort, and assurance. As you read this text, I encourage you to read the scripture references. His Word comes alive when we put it into practice. We can write scriptures down, recite them, and display them. Begin praying the Word during your time with God and applying the Word to your situations. Prayer is powerful, and the Word grants us access to the preeminence of God.

The word 'greater' in the Greek means larger, louder, and bigger than the previous.[1] What is astounding about God is that He supersedes everything that we consider praiseworthy. We can take the most incredible invention, multiply it times a million, and God would still be greater than that! We can't even begin to fathom the height, depth, nor breadth of God in our wildest dreams or imaginations. He is boundless and abundant in every way. If we are going to do greater things then we must be connected to the Great I am. This will require action, prayer, and leadership. When we exercise our faith people can hear, see, and respond to the wondrous ways of our magnificent Father. This task is not meant to fall on the shoulders of one, but many, because the Great Commission requires fellowship and partnership. There is power in connection and strength in numbers.

The Bible records the early church epitomizing the movement of unity in Acts 1:42-47. No one in their midst went without. These believers experienced incomprehensible miracles because everything they did

---

[1] James Strong, *Meizon. In The Strongest Strong's Exhaustive Concordance of the Bible Greek Dictionary-Index to The New Testament* (Grand Rapids: Zondervan, 2001), 3187.

enriched the lives of others. Many sold land and belongings so that all were fed and their needs were met. On top of it all, they had inconceivable joy and favor, and for that reason, people were saved daily.

The first believers were led by the Spirit of God and equipped with holy standards. Every day they sought to know more about God, and they shared with one another through joys and sorrows. Could it be that we are not consistently experiencing miracles on the level of the early church because we are not functioning as they did? The very first group of Christians considered themselves one— the body of Christ. The disciples worked together to achieve the greater things Jesus spoke of by the power of the Holy Spirit. God bestows upon us the same catalyst for miraculous wonders to manifest now. If you are a believer, this power already resides inside of you. How that power is exhibited depends upon your faith, your hope, and the way that you choose to love.

My sincere hope is that as you read this text, you will be encouraged and strengthened in your walk with the LORD. No matter how tough this life can be, you can accomplish greater things through Him when you believe.

Part I

Faith

"Now faith is the assurance of things hoped for,

the conviction of things not seen."

-Hebrews 11:1 (ESV)

What Do You Believe?

Faith is the premise of our entire belief system. The ways in which we think and operate are in direct correlation to what we believe. Faith exists beyond our five senses. We cannot touch, taste, see, smell, or feel faith with our physical body because it is a matter of what we believe in our hearts. Faith contradicts reasoning. This is why groups of very intelligent people have a difficult time embracing the principles of Christianity. Faith supersedes what makes sense. The paradox between faith and facts has the potential to cause someone to lose their trust in Jesus, or never believe in Him at all, but without faith it is impossible to please God. Ephesians 2:8 (ESV) reads,

"For by grace you have been saved through faith. And this is not your own doing; it is the gift of God,"

We are in need of a Savior because of our sins, and this sinfulness is detestable by God. Because of His love for us He gives us the grace necessary to come to Him. There is nothing man-made about the faith it takes to please God. Logic can neither explain it nor attain it, which presents quite a hindrance on those who rely heavily upon their own intellect. Faith does not make sense to the human mind, but as we trust in Him, God will grant us peace that the mind could never produce. The assurance we receive can only come from Him if we believe. As believers, we are aware that we cannot physically see God while on this Earth, but we do trust that He is with us, and that one day we will see Him face to face. Our faith allows us the same perspective in this life. We may not physically see what we are currently hoping for, but we continue to hope until it materializes. Our faith will produce an expectation to receive despite our present circumstances.

The Problem of Evil

Why should I believe in God? Have you ever been faced with this question? In some way or another, we, or those we are connected to, have been impacted by diseases, murders, natural disasters, and other inexplicable horrors that would cause anyone to question their allegiance. One thing we can be sure of is God does not cause evil. One may question the benevolence of God with all of the evil that is present in our society, but there are two things to consider when approaching the problem of evil:

1. God's plans for us are for good (Jeremiah 29:11)
2. God loves us, and has given every individual free will to choose to love Him (Revelation 3:20)

God is perfect and matchless in every way, so why does He love beings that are flawed and disobedient? Consider family members, a spouse, or close friends. Have they ever done or said anything that you disagreed with, or that upset you? Did you stop believing in their existence because of this disagreement? Our parents assisted in our creation, and if they anger us, do we stop believing that they are our parents? Yet this is what happens when people are angry with God. Psalm 139:13 (NLT) reveals,

"You made all the delicate, inner parts of my body and knit me together in my mother's womb."

God is our heavenly Father, and desires to have fellowship with us, which is only possible if we accept Jesus Christ as our personal LORD and Savior. A relationship with Jesus should compel us to put away things that are not in His will for our lives. He wants us to choose Him over the world and all it seemingly has to offer. God is taking a huge risk here. There is a great possibility that we will not choose Him, but when we do, He rejoices (Zephaniah 3:17).

Have you ever felt a yearning for more, and tried to appease it and found that you still weren't satisfied? The longing that we try to fulfill through things in this world always fail because that deep desire can only be satisfied by Him. Throughout scripture He promises never to leave nor forsake us. His Word assures us that He loves and cares for us deeply and compassionately. He is not withholding good things from us, but wants us to come to the realization that everything in the world we think makes us happy pales in comparison to what He has for us. The beauty of His love is found through discovery. When we spend time with Him through Bible reading and prayer, we grow during these times of intimacy with God. Just as it is with a lover, we should continuously take the time to study who He is, learn His ways, and desire to do things that will please Him. When we grow in God, we grow in His love, and exude His love to those around us. Scripture tells us that when we search for Him with all of our heart, we will find Him (Jeremiah 29:13). God romances us, but only to the point where we are willing to be courted.

All of creation has some sort of relationship with God, but the extent of that relationship relies solely on our willingness to cultivate the bond. We have several types of creators in our world—designers, engineers, inventors, scientists, and the like. They manufacture medicines, cars, apparel, and things that assist with everyday life. These people know their product because they created it, and the same applies with God. He uses His expertise to compose beautiful masterpieces, intricately designed for specific tasks in the world. More than anything, He is devoted to His creation, but leaves space for the created to develop intimacy with Him. Every human being who walks on this Earth is connected to God the Father, because He created us, but there are layers to every relationship.

In relationships, we will experience disagreements with our loved ones, and hopefully we try to work it out because we realize how much we care about them and how important they are to us. We move forward in reconciliation because we believe in the good of that union, and the love we have for them. This is a testament to the amount of faith we have in that connection. If we believe that we can work through difficulties, then we demonstrate that what we believe is stronger than what we see or feel.

The same principle applies in our relationship with God. We may not understand why bad things happen, but if He always made things great in our lives, then why would anybody choose not to follow Him? This is something worth noting! If God were a magical genie who performed every miracle we ever asked of Him, we would never revere Him as LORD. If we controlled God with our petitions, He wouldn't be God, He would be our servant. Instead of the one worthy of our reverence, He would be at our disposal, with no regard for His identity or His deity. His rightful place is above all, and He deserves our uncompromising and unwavering devotion.

If Christ sacrificed His life to die a brutal death by crucifixion, which is our deserved punishment as law breakers, the least we could do is lay down our Earthly lives to Him. This exchange grants us eternal life, which last forever, while the turmoil we experience here on Earth is only for a lifetime (2 Corinthians 4:18). This is not meant to reduce the severity of any person's struggle. There is no questioning the devastation we experience while living on this Earth, but we have hope in the promise that one day He will do away with all suffering (Revelation 21:3-5).

Why should God allow us into His kingdom? What makes us appealing to God? If we refer to the twelve disciples of Jesus, most of them were young commoners. Nothing was particularly fascinating about these first followers, and what attributes they did have, our society would deem irrelevant. Any positive human qualities we have will never qualify us for salvation. Without Christ, we lack what is necessary to be in right standing with God.

As we reflect on our own sinfulness, we can recall Judas, who was one of the original twelve disciples. He became a pivotal player in the crucifixion of Christ due to his traitorous actions. In spite of his superficial allegiance to Jesus, we find that Judas had a hidden agenda. The Savior had foreknowledge of this, yet He still called Judas His own and entrusted him with the finances. He treated Judas with the same consideration He had for the other eleven disciples. Why would the Son of God purposefully choose and continue to train one He already knew was going to heinously sin against Him? We know that this was to fulfill the scriptures of Jesus as the Messiah, but there is a portrait of love that will speak for all eternity. The relationship that is depicted in scriptures between Jesus and Judas is a display of a love for a traitor; someone who is unqualified and illegitimate. We all, at some point, have been Judas to Jesus. He poured out His love for Judas the same way He displays His love and affection for us. This transformational love that He displayed well before any of us existed prevails in spite of our denials, doubts, disbelief, and defiance. It is this same love that pressed through a betrayal, and still died for the betrayer. This flawless love continues to love despite our flaws.

Here is something to examine as we move forward: God is God whether we like it or not, and even whether we believe it or not. When we serve and love God despite our feelings, it demonstrates our love for Him. This principle is true even in our Earthly relationships. Relationships are more likely to succeed when both parties are willing to work through the things that are painful. This is not to say that we should succumb to abuse, but rather depend on the grace of God to lead us in the direction that we should go. His desire is for reconciliation.

The statistics for the divorce rate are alarming in our western culture, and it's even more upsetting for Christians! We seem to be under the very false and very sad impression that being a follower of Christ implicates a life free of pain and troubles. This is far from the truth! We are guaranteed troubles in this life (John 16:33), and our adversary works against us hoping that we will forfeit the promises of Christ. When we become hearers and doers of the Word (James 1:22), we gain a capacity for Godly knowledge and truth. Satan uses his best weaponry against us to instigate our demise (John 10:10), but as believers, we have the power to resist him.

Thankfully, God has not only given us weapons and sources of protection (2 Corinthians 10:4-6), but He fights on our behalf (Deuteronomy 3:22). What is most peculiar is that God allows these tests to grow us in our faith. It is odd to think that God uses the worst things in our lives to draw us closer to Him. At any point during these trials we could abandon of our faith, and from a human standpoint, this is a logical alternative. Nevertheless, it is in our most difficult moments that we must turn to the one who has all of the answers. The question should not be, "Why did God allow this to happen?" but rather, "Will I allow my faith to grow in spite of what has happened?"

Belief

John 1:1-5 (NLT) supplies us with an exquisite narrative illuminating the divinity of who Jesus is:

"In the beginning the Word already existed.
The Word was with God,
and the Word was God.
[2] He existed in the beginning with God.
[3] God created everything through him,
and nothing was created except through him.
[4] The Word gave life to everything that was created,
and his life brought light to everyone.
[5] The light shines in the darkness,
and the darkness can never extinguish it."

This is just a portion of the many magnificent attributes of Jesus, and if we are going to have a deeper insight of Christianity, we must understand who Jesus is. Jesus is the Son of God, the Savior of the world, and the Sacrifice for sin. He is a member of the Trinity—God the Father, God the Son, and God the Holy Spirit. The Trinity is not comprised of three different gods, but rather three ways we experience God. Though He is the Messiah, He can only be our Savior when we believe He is the Son.

"This is real love—not that we loved God, but that he loved us and sent his Son as a sacrifice to take away our sins." -1 John 4:10
(NLT)

Loving Jesus means that we will obey His commands (John 14:15). If we love Jesus then we love God, for they are one (John 17). Those who say they love God but do not believe in Jesus are speaking erroneously. You cannot separate the two, for they, along with the Holy Spirit, are one entity. God is a triune being—Father, Son, and Holy Spirit. There is no distinction in the Trinity, for all are God. Some theologians refer to humans as triune beings as well, comprised of a body, soul, and spirit (1 Thessalonians 5:23). Through the power of the Holy Spirit, there is a change that occurs in us during baptism, which is explained in Romans 6:3-6 (NIV):

"Or don't you know that all of us who were baptized into Christ Jesus were baptized into his death? We were therefore buried with him through baptism into death in order that, just as Christ was raised from the dead through the glory of the Father, we too may live a new life. For if we have been united with him in a death like his, we will

certainly also be united with him in a resurrection like his. For we know that our old self was crucified with him so that the body ruled by sin might be done away with, that we should no longer be slaves to sin— because anyone who has died has been set free from sin."

There is great significance in the death and resurrection of Christ Jesus. Our transformation in Christ is a reflection of His resurrection from the dead. Our souls have been redeemed by the blood He shed, and our spirits are infused with His power. Our soul (mind, will, and emotions) is what drives us in our decision making. Our hearts and thoughts are key components in this arena. The spirit is the element that communicates with God. When we give our lives to Christ, we become the resurrection. In order for there to be a resurrection, there must be a death.

We were once sinful creatures driven to do as we pleased until the wonderful love of Christ was revealed to us. This revelation enables us to put immorality to death (Colossians 3:5), and His salvation permits us to live eternally with the King. We die to a life of selfish ambition to become co-heirs with Christ (Romans 8:17). When we die to sinfulness, or become unresponsive to its influence, we are living by the saving grace of Jesus Christ through the power of the Holy Spirit. A resurrected life is epitomized by Galatians 2:20 (ESV):

"I have been crucified with Christ. It is no longer I who live, but Christ who lives in me. And the life I now live in the flesh I live by faith in the Son of God, who loved me and gave himself for me."

This is only possible by faith. Our faith will generate actions that are based on our convictions, and it speaks of what we love. What is poignant about this scripture is that Jesus Christ died for everyone! While He was on this Earth He went to the cross and died for those who cursed Him, beat Him, mocked Him, and ultimately killed Him. As for the present, He died for murderers, thieves, liars, adulterers, gossipers, and the contentious. He died to demonstrate love in its purest form—agape love.

Nothing can ever separate us from His love, but our sins can disconnect us from His presence. This rift is produced by our own inclination to sin. When we walk in darkness, we are taking steps away from the light. God is light, and He overcomes darkness (John 1:5). When we are saved, we come out of the darkness and into His light, which is His presence. He loves us, but He abhors sin and takes no part in it. As a loving Father, He patiently awaits our return (Luke 15:11-32).

In His act of sacrifice, Christ became the only worthy offering for the guilt and stain of sin. In order to appease the wrath that we justly earned, God sent His Son to appease the penalty of sin, which is death. Romans 1:3-4 (NLT) states,

> *The Good News is about his Son. In his earthly life he was born into King David's family line, and he was shown to be the Son of God when he was raised from the dead by the power of the Holy Spirit. He is Jesus Christ our Lord."*

Jesus Christ is a descendant of David, who God promised would have a king on the throne forever (Psalm 89:3-4). His father, Joseph, was from the lineage of Abraham, and His mother, Mary, was pivotal in the incarnation of Christ, by the power of the Holy Spirit. He is of the order of the high priest Melchizedek (Hebrews 5:10), who is known as the king of righteousness. He has the power to heal the sick, raise the dead, cast out demons, and possesses the authority to give this power to others (Matthew 10:1). Above all else, He is LORD. Philippians 2:9-11 tells us that every knee will bow and every tongue will confess that Jesus Christ is LORD.

God confirms the Sonship of Jesus in Matthew 3:17 and in Matthew 17:5. Demons acknowledged that He is the

Son of God and conceded to His authority (Matthew 8:28-34). Jesus has the power to forgive sins and grant us access to the Kingdom of God. If more proof of His divinity is needed, it can be found in how offensive His name is. We cross paths with people who have no problem speaking about God, but may become indignant if Jesus is mentioned. God is frequently reduced to a 'higher power.' This is socially acceptable because this 'higher power' can be interpreted however one chooses to do so. Nevertheless, there is no question about who Jesus is, and scripture confirms this. Even history records His miraculous power, which makes it extremely difficult to refute His deity.

The Bible uses very strong and powerful language about submission and lowliness, and this goes against every facet of our being. Our society teaches us that we should do what we want, when we want, and nobody has the right to tell us that our behavior is wrong. In the Kingdom of God, submission is power, because we concede to the strength of God, which surpasses all things. With His power over sin, He also conquered death. The spiritual death caused by sin has been conquered through Christ (Romans 6:23). John 12:44 tells us that if we believe in God, then we must believe in Jesus, because God sent Him to become the Savior.

Everything Jesus did while on Earth was a manifestation of the will of the Father. It is not possible to believe in God the Father, but fail to acknowledge God the Son. In doing so, we condemn ourselves by our disbelief (John12:44-50). Therefore, it is not God who sends people to hell, but a lack of faith that prohibits entrance into heaven. Some may retort the Omni-benevolence of God, countering that if God is so good, why is there a hell? In efforts to combat these contentions, some Christians focus solely on the loving and just attributes of God. John 3:16 is a very commonly used verse to draw people to Christ, and it enlightens us of the personage of the atonement for our sins. Yet, we must explore the proceeding verses. John 3:18 (ESV) states,

"Whoever believes in him is not condemned, but whoever does not believe is condemned already, because he has not believed in the name of the only Son of God."

There are two very important components to this: to believe and to be condemned. When we believe in Jesus, we trust Him, and because of that trust, our actions will exhibit our faith. When we believe, we will not be condemned because our actions line up with our faith. However, if we choose not to believe in Christ, we are already condemned. The term 'condemned' in the Greek means to determine one thing to be greater, or better than another. [2] In essence, to not choose Christ is to choose the world, and to choose the world is to pass judgment that Jesus is not the Messiah. It is our own beliefs and subsequent actions that either acquit or condemn us.

Scripture substantiates that Jesus did not come into the world to condemn us. For example, we can investigate the story of the woman caught in adultery. According to the Law of Moses, the penalty for this sin was to be stoned to death in a public area. The humiliation was a lesson for the masses, but the death was the penalty for the sin. Upon arriving on the scene and told of the incident, Jesus communicated that whoever was without sin could throw the first stone. All of the accusers left, and Jesus utters these beautiful words in John 8:10-11 (NLT),

> *"...Then Jesus stood up again and said to the woman, "Where are your accusers? Didn't even one of them condemn you?"*
>
> *"No, Lord," she said.*
>
> *And Jesus said, "Neither do I. Go and sin no more."*

---

[2] James Strong, *Krino. In The Strongest Strong's Exhaustive Concordance of the Bible Greek Dictionary-Index to The New Testament* (Grand Rapids: Zondervan, 2001), 2919.

The same compassion is exhibited to us when we choose to follow Him. When our accuser, Satan, comes to condemn us, Jesus has the final answer. The wages of sin is death, but the debts of all believers have been paid. Furthermore, Jesus gives us authority over our sin, and Romans 8:3-4 (NLT) illustrates this concept:

> "*The law of Moses was unable to save us because of the weakness of our sinful nature. So God did what the law could not do. He sent his own Son in a body like the bodies we sinners have. And in that body God declared an end to sin's control over us by giving his Son as a sacrifice for our sins. He did this so that the just requirement of the law would be fully satisfied for us, who no longer follow our sinful nature but instead follow the Spirit.*"

We must perceive the difference between habitual sins and stumbling in many ways. Habitual sin means a dependency has formed and a deliberate and repetitive action occurs because of it. Some may be aware that this habit is detrimental, yet are struggling to overcome it. Some may not realize that their actions are harmful, or may be convinced that nothing is wrong with their behavior. When we fall short, the unredeemed parts of us dictate our conduct. It is human nature to succumb to fleshly desires when we are tired, hungry, lonely, or angry. These temperaments encourage decisions that will appease our flesh, which could lead to sin. To combat this, we rely on the Spirit (Romans 8:12-14).

A very common question people will ask is, "How do I stop sinning?" The truth is we don't have that ability apart from Christ. When we fully give our lives over to God, the tendency to sin lessens. We become more and more like the one we make a habit of following. We can stop ourselves from making sin a lifestyle by the power of the Holy Spirit. Jesus has given us the capacity for renewed lives regardless of our past indiscretions. The only way out of a life of sin is a life that is in Christ. This does not mean that we will never sin again, but it does mean that we have the ability to live righteously despite our sinful inclinations.

"Those who belong to Christ Jesus have crucified the flesh with its passions and desires. Since we live by the Spirit, let us keep in step with the Spirit." -Galatians 5:24-25 (NIV)

We have the power to resist the desires that do not lead to godliness. In Him, we have all that we need to overcome temptation. We conquer sin and ultimately spiritual death by living in Him, and allowing Him to work in us. *"And I am sure of this, that he who began a good work in you will bring it to completion at the day of Jesus Christ."* -Philippians 1:6 (ESV)

Just as Jesus conquered sin, He also conquered death. Romans 6:23 tells us that the penalty for sin is death, yet it is a death we will never experience if we believe in the Son. Romans 6:1-4 illuminates that the power of Christ frees us from the grasp of sin. He demolished the control sin had over us so that once we believe we are no longer obligated to act according to our sinful nature. His physical death gave us power over spiritual death. It can be difficult to talk about sin, but it shouldn't be avoided. If we ignore issues of the heart and mind, we will never be able to conquer them, and eventually, they will conquer us. It is by the blood of the Lamb and the word of our testimonies that we overcome (Revelation 12:11).

God does forgive us of our sin, but it is not acceptable for us to continually walk in error when we know our actions are wrong (James 4:17). Some may refrain from teaching the severity of sin because of fear of losing friends or church members, but it is the responsibility of the body of Christ to teach the truth, regardless of what the social norm might be (2 Timothy 4:3). A life in Christ requires surrendering to His authority. An honest evaluation should take place to perceive who is really in control of our lives. If we make decisions without consulting our Savior, we are choosing to live a life that is less than the one Christ died to provide for us.

One of the most incredible promises about making a decision to follow Jesus is that one day He will do away with all pain, suffering, and turmoil (Revelation 21:4). It is true that God heals, protects, and provides, but we must understand that we have not only aligned ourselves with the most powerful Being, but we have also enlisted into an army. Every successful army has training, and our training is spiritual. Every army also has an enemy, and our enemy is Satan.

When soldiers enlist into the military, they are agreeing to the terms of the armed forces. Usually, this involves strict physical and mental training, as well as a disciplined and rigid schedule. There is much instruction, preparation, exercise, and disciplining needed to prepare for war. Regardless of the occupational specialty a soldier signs up for, the common goal for every fighter is to win battles. Combatants must be ready to go to war at any moment, regardless of what they were doing with their family or at their usual place of business. As long as they are a soldier, they are expected to fight. In our Christian life we fight spiritual battles against an enemy that is notorious for distorting truth and attacking us with adversity.

It is a common, yet poor misconception to think that entering the faith will eliminate every aspect of suffering. This mindset of perfection must be destroyed because it is one of the devil's most crafty ideas. The notion that Jesus will offer you a life free of pain while living on this Earth causes distrust when those moments come. Yes, He does enrich our lives far more than we could ever dream, but as long as we live, our faith will be tested. Some turn away from the faith, or refuse to believe because they have taken this bait from Satan. Despite the trials of this life, we are assured great triumphs, victory, and exceeding joy.

"Consider it pure joy, my brothers and sisters, whenever you face trials of many kinds, because you know that the testing of your faith produces perseverance. Let perseverance finish its work so that you may be mature and complete, not lacking anything." -James 1:2-4 (NIV)

We do not serve a God who does not know what it is like to resist temptation. Matthew 4:1-11 explicates the enticements Jesus overcame. We see that after He fasted, the Spirit of God led Jesus into the wilderness to be tempted. Why would God allow His Son to be tested by His enemy? There are a few things that set the stage here for a remarkable story. The text reveals that Jesus fasted for 40 days and 40 nights. In this state of extreme hunger and fatigue He was susceptible to much. Many are aware of the hunger pangs and listlessness that comes from a lack of nourishment. Secondly, He was in the wilderness—a place that is filled with danger, unfamiliarity, and uncertainty. Jesus could have been attacked by various types of beasts and plagued by intense weather conditions. On top of it all, He was encountered by the most heinous criminal in the entire world.

Why did God allow Jesus to be tested? We can infer that God allowed His Son to be tested because He allows us to be tested. What better model of success than Christ? Everything Satan tries to devise against us is a tactic to take our focus off of our faith and onto our feelings. First John 2:16-17 (NIV) conveys,

"For everything in the world—the lust of the flesh, the lust of the eyes, and the pride of life—comes not from the Father but from the world. The world and its desires pass away, but whoever does the will of God lives forever."

Towards the end of His fast, Jesus was hungry, so Satan sought to get Him to provide for Himself by turning stones into bread. Would He break His fast to prove that He could provide for Himself? He was hungry, after all, and would be justified in doing so. If Satan was tempting Him to do it, obviously it was not the will of the Father. Jesus refused, knowing that a greater good would come because of this sacrifice. Christ knew He had power, but understood that it was not for His own benefit. His life was meant to be poured out for the glorification of God and for the sanctification of mankind. In this, Jesus overcame the lust of the flesh.

In his next attempt, Satan asked Jesus to throw Himself down, and even quoted scripture about how the Father would save Him! Satan was tempting Jesus to focus on His status by challenging him with the following phrase: "prove you are the Son of God." Jesus knew that He was the Son of God, but Satan was questioning His identity. For us, there will be moments in life when others will try to minimize our qualities. It can feel like an overbearing temptation to defend ourselves when contrary words are spoken against us. Jesus knew better than to test the LORD, and left the substantiation of His deity in the hands of His Father. In this, He surmounted the pride of life.

Lastly, Satan flashed the kingdoms of this world and all its glory before His eyes and said it could all belong to Jesus if He would bow down and worship him. Jesus was already King—He left His thrown to save humanity. The avenue back to His Kingdom was filled with inconceivable pain that generated every negative human emotion possible. What Satan was offering would have been easier, presumably painless, and included the riches of this world. Yet Jesus understood where His dedication resided, and it was not with the antagonist of heaven and Earth. Imagine knowing you were going to suffer a gruesome death, and being offered a way out. There is no doubting the weight of temptation to bow out of the will of God. Still, Jesus understood His purpose, even if He didn't want to endure the pain. He desired the will of God more than His own physical well-being. In this, Jesus conquered the lust of the eyes.

These same tactics are used against us now, and God the Father allowed Jesus to be tested so that we would know how to resist our enemy. We must familiarize ourselves with the ploys of Satan, and be cognizant that right in the middle of the word SIN is 'I'. If comfort is our driving force in the decision making process, we offer a passageway for the enemy to wreak havoc in our lives. Satan wants to rob us of our dependence on God, eliminate our opportunities for spiritual growth, and dismantle our allegiance with God by enticing us with worldly pleasures. Sin is insatiable, and the more we give into temptation, the more desensitized we will become to its harmful effects. We have been redeemed back to God, and because of our redemption, victory, power, and truth rightfully belong to us. This world and all of its pleasures will pass away, so it is in our best interest to pursue an everlasting covenant with the Father.

Our lives are filled with choices, and our freedom of choice is not taken away once we become Christians. The depth of our relationship with Christ is dependent upon our desire for Him. We can have as much, or as little of God as we want. If we make the choice to go deeper, we must accept the dangers. We are at risk of losing friends and loved ones who do not understand and suffer persecution in various arenas of our lives. When truly growing in Christ, we come face to face with our temperaments that are offensive to God, and we will find ourselves being challenged by less than lovely circumstances.

The book of James admonishes us to put on joy in these circumstances because whenever we are going through trials, there is an opportunity for improvement. We can relate this to physical training. If we do the same workout every day for a week, and eat healthier foods, we are likely to see improvements. If we do not add intensity or change the variables of our workouts, we will eventually plateau. The workout regimen should change so that we continue to challenge the body. If we fail to do this, working out will eventually seem mundane, and we will become stagnant as the body becomes accustomed to the training. We were created to adapt and overcome, and this is exactly what happens when we train. If we lift the same 15 pound weight in the same way every day, after a while we will not see the results that once motivated us to continue working out. The same is true for our spiritual well-being. If we do nothing more than read the same passage of scripture and pray the same words in the same manner every day for weeks on end, we will eventually become unresponsive and indifferent about the things that once brought us so much joy and excitement. Instead of being defeated, the result will be a forfeit.

The price of following Christ is costly, but the choice not to will accumulate a debt we can never repay.

When we profess Christ, some friendships will fade, family members may distance themselves, we may be labeled extremists, or find ourselves defending our faith to strangers. Still, none of the sufferings we endure during our lifetime can ever compare to the glorious eternity we will spend in heaven (Romans 8:18). The alternative to following Christ is not just physical and eternal death in hell, but separation from God. Every person on the Earth has a connection to God, but in order to be saved, we must have a relationship with God.

All humans are His creation, but not all of us are His people. There are two powers at war for our souls, and one of them uses the bait of this world (money, sex, fame, and power) to suppress us in darkness. The other chooses the light of truth, mercy, and love to accomplish greater works that money can never acquire. Material wealth can never purchase the peace or joy that comes from God or the promise of absolute fulfillment at the coming of Christ. Yes, money grants us more choices and options, but it can never fill the void that can only be satisfied by Christ. This is why scripture warns us about the love of money (1Timothy 6:6-10).

Although Jesus is divine, He became one of us, meaning that He was clothed in human frailty. What is the importance of this truth? If we consider the humanity, as well as the divinity of Jesus, we recognize that He had the power to save Himself, but He chose to suffer so that we could be free from the power of sin. We find in Romans 8:3 that the Law of Moses was unable to save us because of our sinful nature. Therefore, God sent His Son down from heaven to accomplish what the law failed to do, and it is because of Jesus that we receive liberty from the bondage of sin. Once we accept Christ we are no longer under the obligation to satisfy our sinful nature. This does not mean there is no purpose for the Law, for the law shows us how we fall short of the standards of God. Rules and regulations are put into place to keep us safe from harm, but at any moment in time we can see, hear, or read about theft, arson, murder, and the like. The law shows us how corrupt humanity is, but Jesus delivers us out of destitution.

Any person who is willing to reflect over the moments in their lives can say unequivocally that there were times that they deserved some sort of punishment. Here we embark upon another inconceivable truth about God's love and mercy. God sent His holy Son to become flesh and live on the Earth. During His lifetime He experienced the same torment, hardship, pain, and temptation we are subjected to, yet He remained blameless.

As He was beaten, bruised, and nailed to the cross, He paid the price for every crime that had ever, and would ever, be committed.

We can probably imagine suffering for the wrong we have committed, but what about suffering for the sins of strangers, or worse, those who have mistreated us? Jesus was a man who was beyond reproach, and yet He assumed responsibility for the penalty of every sinner, every law breaker, and every perpetrator. He was beaten, tortured, ridiculed, abandoned, betrayed, and murdered for transgressions He did not commit. Before Christ, there were several sacrificial rituals that required flawless animals, and these requirements could only be performed by a priest. The death of Jesus was the final sacrifice, fulfilling the law in its entirety (Hebrews 10).

We tend to focus on the physical pain and suffering Jesus experienced before his death, but not much is mentioned about why his fear of the cross was so great. Yes, Jesus was aware that He would suffer for sins He did not commit, but more than anything, Jesus dreaded the separation from God He would experience in the time between His death and resurrection. We too, should be apprehensive at the thought of being separated from God's presence. In this state, we are detached from His grace that protects us, His strength that fights for us, and His mercy that keeps us. This should be more feared than any unthinkable horror we can imagine.

Jesus experienced very similar situations to what we encounter, yet he never sinned. Before salvation, there are behaviors that are socially acceptable. After salvation, the Holy Spirit comes to live inside of us, guiding us as we allow Him to. Old behaviors, habits, and thinking patterns change for the better, and morality becomes a governing thought. John 14:16-17 (NIV) states,

"If you love me, keep my commands. And I will ask the Father, and he will give you another advocate to help you and be with you forever—the Spirit of truth. The world cannot accept him, because it neither sees him nor knows him. But you know him, for he lives with you and will be in you."

Before Christ, we are under the authority of the god of this world who is known as the "father of lies" (John 8:44). After Christ, we are under the authority of God, but we continue to live in a world governed by Satan. We are no longer under the rule of Satan even though we still reside where he has power. His power does not reign over Christians, it only affects us. Nevertheless, Christ has overcome the world (John 16:33). One of the many lies of

Satan is that if we are a good person, God won't send us to hell. Even if we met every human criteria of a 'good person,' it doesn't make us good enough to fulfill the standards of a holy God. What makes us good is accepting Jesus Christ as our LORD and Savior.

To live righteously in a world full of wickedness we must adhere to the truth taught to us by the Holy Spirit (John 16:8-11). The Holy Spirit convicts us, and gives us the ability to walk in righteousness, but he does not take away our ability to sin. If He did, our free-will would be removed and we would no longer have the power to choose. God wants us to choose Him, but if He makes us choose Him, it would be a dictatorship and not a relationship. Yet, He shows His love and faithfulness by gracing us with His Holy Spirit. Because of His guidance, we are no longer under the compulsion to sin. However, if we are submitting to our sinful nature more than we are allowing the Holy Spirit to guide us, the result will be immorality. This is evident in Galatians 5:16-25.

How can we expect to be like Jesus if He is God? Though He is God, His fleshly nature gave Him the ability to sin. Despite His capacity to do wrong, He remained blameless. He was divinity enveloped in humanity so that He could relate to a perishing world. Our society esteems greatness, and we are more apt to follow someone we have a common bond with. This man, who was also God, gave up His prestige and His throne in heaven to come to Earth to demonstrate to the world that He loves us.

Our culture teaches us to be driven by achievement. We need to be successful so that we can make more money and have more things. Not many would relinquish their prominence for people who didn't believe in them, or lay down their lives for manipulators and imposters. Yet this is exactly what Christ did. He disregarded His status to become the sacrifice for the very people who blatantly disrespect and disregard His name. He did it all to show us what love really means.

How is Jesus like us? How can imperfect people ever be associated with a perfect God? In human form, Jesus had physical needs: He grew, He became frustrated, He cried, He learned, and He was also tempted. We cannot be tempted by something we do not have a desire for. If someone does not like chocolate then placing a plate of it in front of them would not be alluring. When scriptures teach that Jesus was tempted, we must recognize that in His humanity, He had the ability to yield to these temptations. Jesus prevailed as the victor because His desire to please His Father was greater than His inclination for the pleasures of this world.

As the god of this world (2 Corinthians 4:4), Satan has the ability to give the things of this world. The enemy's power is a counterfeit imitation of the absolute power of God. In fact, Paul writes in 2 Corinthians 11:14-15 (NIV),

"And no wonder, for Satan himself masquerades as an angel of light. It is not surprising, then, if his servants also masquerade as servants of righteousness. Their end will be what their actions deserve."

Throughout scripture, we find that we have an enemy who will do everything he can to cause us to acquire the same fate he has. Every inhabitant on Earth is caught in the midst of a battle between good and evil, but the people of God are called to withstand. The meaning of 'withstand' in the Greek is to resist, rebel, and oppose.[3] Second Corinthians 10:4-6 teaches us that our weapons are not physical, and Ephesians 6:12 communicates that our enemies are not made of flesh. We fight by identifying the lies and replacing them with the truth of God's Word.

---

[3] James Strong, *Anthistemi. In The Strongest Strong's Exhaustive Concordance of the Bible Greek Dictionary-Index to The New Testament* (Grand Rapids: Zondervan, 2001), 436.

Typically, when a fight is mentioned, combat comes to mind. In combat there is a display of strength and power. In the Kingdom of God, we are called to surrender. We do not concede to our opponent, but to the one who makes us strong. When we yield to God, we give Him dominion over our situations, and He fights on our behalf (Deuteronomy 20:4). When we stand, we make a declaration to Satan that we are a force to be reckoned with by the power of the LORD. It is our trust in God that brings victory into our lives (Ephesians 6:10-18). Standing does not mean we do nothing. When we stand in God, we take a posture of confidence in Him to destroy the enemy on our behalf. However, there is still work to be done. It is our responsibility to read, pray, fast, act, believe, and speak the word of God over our situations. For everything that is beyond our ability, we place our unwavering dependence on Him. When we are hurt by someone, it is very easy to identify them as a foe, but people are not our adversaries. There are spirits operating behind the actions of people, and this is just one of Satan's devious ways to cause division and strife. When we are hurt by the actions of others, we must direct our battle tactics against Satan, not man.

One thing we can be sure of with Christ is that we will not be tempted beyond our ability to resist. During the temptation, God always offers us a way of escape (1 Corinthians 10:13). Television has portrayed the classic crossroad of good and evil with an angel on one shoulder, and a demon on the other giving advice to a person about which decision to make. This is very similar to what happens in our minds when fighting temptation. The ability to do good and evil resides within us. What we give more thought to is what will prevail. What we immerse ourselves in is what will prosper. If we abide in holiness, holiness will triumph. If we abide in wickedness, then wickedness will prevail. To overcome temptation, all we have to do is make the decision not to sin. In 2 Timothy 2:22 (ESV) we are admonished to,

"...flee youthful passions and pursue righteousness, faith, love, and peace, along with those who call on the LORD from a pure heart."

We cannot simply ask God to help us stop sinning. We must be willing to walk out the personal and social aspects of that freedom. In the game of tag, there is a 'tagger' who is 'it' and everyone else runs away from this person trying not to be tagged. The 'tagger' attempts to get rid of the title by chasing others down. The same principle can be applied in our spiritual lives. We run away from things that do not exemplify righteousness, and run towards that which pleases Him. Righteous living is the product of the fruit of the Spirit—love, joy, peace, patience, kindness, goodness, faithfulness, gentleness, and self-control (Galatians 5:22-23).

Jesus commanded us to love one another. If all people loved God, others, and ourselves the way the Word instructs us to, there would be no sin in the world. First John 4:7-8 instructs believers to love one another because if we belong to God we will love like He loves, and love does no wrong to its neighbor. Walking in love is the fulfillment of the law (Romans 13:10).

Without faith, it is impossible to please God. We will not please God, nor will we have the desire to, unless we have cultivated a relationship with Him. Christianity is not a religion of rules that make us good enough, because Jesus is enough. We are not governed by regulations, but we are directed by love, and love is the fulfillment of all that is good. The level of our intimacy with God relies entirely on our willingness to be vulnerable with Him. We can have as much or as little of God as we choose, though it is His desire that we would choose the former. Our faith gives us access to Jesus. After we receive Him as our Savior, the Holy Spirit dwells within us, guiding us in the way that we should go, but only as far as we are willing.

When we come to the end of this life, we will discover that we ultimately had two options for our eternity—heaven or hell. What we choose to believe is a product of free will. If we choose to be reliant on the LORD, our lives will reflect His glory. When we pray the powerful words Jesus uttered moments before His arrest, "Not my will, but yours be done," we enter into a realm of endless possibilities. Our faith depends on a trust that has to be persistent and consistent. Our belief in the promises of God reverses what it unrealistic, unattainable, and unachievable. We base our faith on what we hope to see, and will see, if we believe. That is the paradox of the Christian faith—to believe in what is unbelievable.

He replied, "Because you have so little faith. Truly I tell you, if you have faith as small as a mustard seed, you can say to this mountain, 'Move from here to there,' and it will move. Nothing will be impossible for you."

-Matthew 17:20 (NIV)

Part II

Hope

"...the LORD *delights in those who fear him,*

who put their hope in his unfailing love."

-Psalm 147:11(NIV)

In the Midst of Pain

"Father, if you are willing, take this cup from me; yet not my will, but yours be done." An angel from heaven appeared to him and strengthened him. And being in anguish, he prayed more earnestly, and his sweat was like drops of blood falling to the ground."

-Luke 22:42-44 (NIV)

Before His arrest, Jesus prayed fervently that the Father would allow the cup of wrath to pass Him, yet He surrendered by saying, "Not my will, but yours be done." Jesus knew His purpose but He struggled with His emotions to carry out the plan. Despite His emotions, Jesus loved His Father more than His own life. In His surrender, He aligned Himself with the will of the Father. As He submitted Himself in obedience, God sent an angel to give Him the strength to do what He felt like He could not do. When Jesus realized that He had been strengthened, He prayed even more fervently, but there is no mention of anymore prayers for mercy.

Even Jesus struggled with the will of God, but He overcame that struggle by trusting in the Father. Yes, God heard His cry for mercy, but He responded by giving Jesus what He needed, not what He wanted. Jesus felt 'the cup' was too much for Him to bear, but in spite of His feelings, He submitted in obedience, and God trusted Him to become the Savior of the universe! When Jesus took His eyes off of the things He would suffer, He was able to bear the will of God. God will never strengthen us to carry out our own plans when He has already given us directives to fulfill His.

Matthew 11:30 tells us that His yoke is easy and His burden is light. 'Yoke' is a term used for farming. It is a wooden tool that connects two animals together to carry a heavy load. God doesn't just ask us to do His will, He comes along beside us applying His power and sharing in our suffering. We have the assurance of Christ that if we suffer now, we will share in His glory later (Romans 8:17). He is our power and we are His vessels. Without His power our efforts would be futile, but without the vessel, there is only potential. This is not to reduce the effects of the power of the LORD. Potential power is a ramification of an immense capability that is in need of a conduit. Without an instrument the power cannot be sourced. We will not see the manifestation of His power in our lives if we neglect to fulfill His will.

If we fail to realize our purpose we will become instruments without use. A vacuum that is intended to clean dirty carpets, but is never used does not change the fact that it is still a vacuum cleaner. However, the effects of unclean carpets could result in vermin or health issues, and a more expensive tool must be used or the carpet must be replaced. The original intent of the vacuum cleaner was to maintain the carpet. The alternative action could have been avoided if the vacuum was used in the first place. Once the vacuum is plugged in and used, its purpose is being fulfilled. The carpet receives its necessary maintenance and everyone who lives in the house benefits. The same is true in our Christian walk. If we never do what God has specifically designed for our lives, it does not change His purpose, but it does change our impact. God is looking for willing vessels to deposit His power so that His purposes can be accomplished.

God may require us to do or go through things that are painful physically, psychologically, or emotionally, but it is never without purpose. Our understanding of God is limited, and we may not be able to comprehend the reason for these events until later. We know that in some capacity, His people will benefit, whether it is spiritual growth, a testimony to the world, or other rationales that we cannot fathom. Above all, we must recognize that His desire is to display His glory through His people. First Peter 3:14 (NLT) reads,

"But even if you suffer for doing what is right, God will reward you for it. So don't worry or be afraid of their threats."

We are chosen to be instruments in the overarching plan for humanity. However, if we never say yes, we will never be sourced. The gift of salvation is available to all, but gifts can only be given if they are received. The reception, or lack thereof, does not change the intent of the giver, but it does reveal the heart of the intended receiver.

In light of why we are tested, we can refer to 1 Peter 1:6-8. There are two opposing forces warring for our allegiance. God allows testing to strengthen us while Satan uses testing to upset us. God wants us to depend on a power that is greater than our own, while Satan engrosses us with thoughts of self-sufficiency. God wants us to be successful and faithful, and Satan tries to usurp this with attacks. In these moments of testing, we are acquitted or condemned by what we do and do not believe.

There are several ways to overcome the tactics of the enemy. First, James 1:5 tells us to ask for wisdom.

Before all else we should seek the face of God and ask for the wisdom that comes from heaven (James 3:17). When we find ourselves in the middle of a test, the two possible outcomes are pass or fail. If we're not asking for assistance from God, then it can be presumed that we are not properly equipped to engage in battle. To ignore the war that is being waged against us spiritually is comparable to being in a boxing ring with an opponent and turning our back to him. Just because we don't acknowledge what is happening doesn't mean it isn't happening or that it will go away. Ignorance is not bliss in spiritual matters. In fact, ignorance is willingly putting on a blindfold and becoming target practice for the enemy.

Wisdom is a gift from God, which He freely gives when we ask. James 1:5-8 advises that we will only receive if our faith is in God alone. True wisdom can only come from God, and this wisdom promotes action, which is why the verses instruct us to believe that we already have what we are asking for. When we are confident and bold in our faith, we trust that we will possess what we have requested. This position of faith is not out of a sense of entitlement, but an understanding that the Father blesses us because He is faithful. We are undeserving recipients of God's unmerited favor and grace. There cannot be faith without works, so once we ask for wisdom and receive it, our response should be faithful action. If we act like we have the promise, we will eventually obtain it.

A lack of wisdom will be characterized by irresponsible decision making. James 1:6 admonishes us to have faith and not doubt because a man who doubts is like a wave of the sea, being tossed around by the wind. Waves are unpredictable because the wind causes them to rise and fall, crash violently, or reach the shore with calm. When we doubt, we are allowing disbelief to cause us to be unpredictable and erratic. If we keep our minds on Him, He will keep us in perfect peace (Isaiah 26:3). Asking for and being guided by wisdom, guards us from imprudent decisions and behaviors.

We can always expect to have victory through Christ no matter what life may bring us. However, the outcome may look very different from what we expect. During our lifetime we will lose loved ones, personal belongings, and may not obtain things we had hoped for. These unfavorable circumstances can come even after we pray, fast, and remain hopeful. This and other tragedies have the potential to create susceptibility to a doubting mentality. No one can know the mind and heart of God well enough to see how the Creator of the Universe formulates all that exists and causes it to operate. We cannot explain why dreadful things occur, but despite the pain and agony this life may bring, we know that everything works for our good when we love God and are called according to His purpose (Romans 8:28). In Isaiah 55:8-9 (ESV) we find the following encouragement,

"For my thoughts are not your thoughts, neither are your ways my ways," declares the LORD. "For as the heavens are higher than the Earth, so are my ways higher than your ways and my thoughts than your thoughts."

We are confident that one day all suffering will end forever because our hope rests on the one who conquered death (1 Corinthians 15:55-57). Although we acknowledge Him as omnipotent, some of our life experiences will cause us to question His existence, benevolence, and willingness to help us. Pain can come through various circumstances, but several of our hurts come from people. Divorce, infidelity, abuse, theft, and the like can produce skepticism. Because of free will, people have the ability to help and hurt us. The depth of our relationships with others does not make them incapable of causing us pain. In fact, it is often those who are closest to us that hurt us the most.

During these trials and hardships, we have two options: lose hope and allow the pain to absorb our world, or fight back and trust that a greater good will come as a result of our faithfulness and hopefulness. Every individual has the right to choose, however, that choice may not lead to the most desirable outcome. There are many stories of triumph in the face of adversity, but victories do not come without opposition. We will gain so much if we can press on towards the mark (Philippians 3:14). If marriages can be restored and familial relationships repaired, then our faith and trust in God should outlast our circumstances. We cannot trust people more than the one who created them. Romans 5:3-5 (NIV) asserts,

"Not only so, but we also glory in our sufferings, because we know that suffering produces perseverance; perseverance, character; and character, hope. And hope does not put us to shame, because God's love has been poured out into our hearts through the Holy Spirit, who has been given to us."

Perseverance is the foundation of patience. Patience produces contentment that assures us as we wait. During this time, we are given the opportunity to show what we truly believe. If we persevere, we prove that we believe that God will provide for us. Our hope is built with confidence and expectation, being sure of what we are waiting for, and convinced that we will receive it. If we exhibit a lack of patience, then it is evident that we also have a lack of hope. You cannot have hope without first having patience.

Patience in the Word of God is known as 'long-suffering.' Many associate this with being able to suffer for a long time, but it is also a demonstration of the right attitude for an extended period of time, especially when the wait is longer than expected. A person who has the fruit of the spirit characterized by long-suffering is not easily moved by emotions, because he or she demonstrates self-control and restraint in spite of those difficult feelings. We have the assurance that no matter the circumstance, the strength we need can always be found in Christ (Philippians 4:13).

Hope in the Promise

One thing believers must remember is that Jesus
Christ loved us so much that He endured the worst so that
we could experience everlasting joy and salvation (Romans
5:6-8). The alternative is eternal separation from God
which brings destitution, deprivation, and hell. We can be
sure that once we have accepted the gift of eternal life
through Jesus that we have security in the promise, despite
the pain this life might produce. Here we can return to our
conversation of sin and salvation. Paul wrote to the
Galatians about their desire to uphold the law after
professing Christ. The problem was not that these
Galatians wanted to be 'good,' but they were using noble
behavior as a method to obtain salvation.

In the text, Paul is referring to the law of the
Pentateuch, which is upheld in Judaism. These are
regulations that were originally intended to bring mankind
back into right standing with God. As mentioned before,
there were sacrifices that needed to be made during
specific times of the year, and a priest had to conduct the
ceremonies for these sacrifices. However, once Jesus
sacrificed His life on the cross, there was no longer a need
for a priest to mediate between God and man because Jesus

satisfied the law with His death. In addition to this, Jesus is now our intercessor, who sits at the right hand of the Father (Romans 8:34). Paul admonished the Galatians that if righteousness could be attained by works, there would have been no reason for Jesus to die on the cross (Galatians 2:21). We must understand that Christ is the fulfillment of the law. The law was given to show us our sin. If we didn't have the law, we wouldn't know that we needed God. With knowledge comes responsibility. We can reference the fall of man in the Garden of Eden to gain a deeper understanding of this concept.

In the third chapter of Genesis, there is an account of the serpent, the craftiest of all beings. He convinced Eve to eat from the Tree of Knowledge of Good and Evil. She was aware that God commanded them not to eat from the tree, and conveys this information to the serpent. Somehow he is still able to persuade her to go against the command spoken by God. She not only eats the fruit, but offers some to her husband. There are a few things that we must acknowledge about this record. First, God gives us free will so that we can make a conscious and whole-hearted decision to serve Him. He wants our love for Him to be genuine, fostered by real emotions that produce an everlasting relationship.

Second, as much as there is an ever-present God on our side, there is a cunning adversary that seeks to destroy us. Genesis 3 chronicles how the enemy makes lies appear as truth. Satan has been fated for eternal damnation for his pride. Instead of wanting to serve God, he wanted to be served as god, and his arrogance led to his demise. Along with him followed a legion of angels that joined his campaign. They now serve as his imps in eternal damnation (Revelation 12:9). He aims for us to have the same fate, and does everything within his power to ensnare us. This is why he is known as the deceiver, and his objective is to cause us to believe what is counterfeit (2 Corinthians 11:3).

He takes every truth and perverts it for his benefit. What makes him successful in distorting the truth is how he poses the lies to those he is trying to deceive. He presents things that could possibly be true, while appealing to our desires. Satan observes to see what we like, what frustrates us, and what causes us to stumble. He learns our weaknesses and even knows our strengths. What is the biggest lie Satan tells? From this account in the Garden of Eden, we can resolve that Satan's ultimate plan is to make us believe that we can be our own god.

In Genesis 1:26-28 God created Adam and Eve and gave them dominion over the Earth. He fashioned a male and a female in His image and His likeness, and gave them authority over things on the Earth. God has called us to be like Him, but He never says that we are to be gods. This is the same falsehood that Satan deceived himself into believing, and it is the same fallacious concept he uses to deceive us.

As we progress in Christ, we discover that God is in control. He has a power greater than anything this world could ever produce. We may not realize it, but we seek control in our everyday lives and interactions with others. We want to know what happens next, and we take the necessary steps to secure ideologies and possessions we believe will lead to or display our successes. When we get into disagreements, we want the other party to realize our point and concede that we are correct. Our daily plight is to have power over our day and command every moment. We want to be the masters of our schedules, our moods, our affections, and our desires. This is the same power struggle that Satan had in heaven. He wanted to be in control and lusted after the power that only God can possess and manage. Satan wanted what did not belong to him, and for that reason, he and a multitude of other angels were thrown into the pit of hell.

Our adversary attempts to manipulate us against the knowledge we have of God. There are several passages of scripture that detail the enemy, and often his method of attack is through people. John 10:10 (NIV) describes how he wars against us:

"The thief comes only to steal and kill and destroy; I have come that they may have life, and have it to the full."

This piece of evidence is also clear in the story of the fall of man. Satan baited Eve, who later drew in Adam. Satan used Eve, whom Adam loved, to defy the one Adam should have loved the most. While being confronted by God, Adam shifted blame to Eve, who then accused the serpent, yet, the serpent was quiet. When facing God, Satan will forever stand condemned as our defeated foe.

A typical response when a trespass is being exposed is to find fault in others. A mature response is to look inward and take responsibility for our actions. Satan will entice us to blame others because this conduct hinders spiritual growth. The truth of the matter lies in the heart, and God knows the spiritual condition of us all. We cannot focus solely on the symptoms; we must get to the root of the issue if we want to cure the sickness. Treating the symptoms without treating the illness doesn't cure the disease; it only temporarily masks the problem. In order to diminish the symptoms we have to get to the root of the problem.

Pride was the issue in the fall of man. Eve was inclined to eat of the Tree of Knowledge of Good and Evil because she thought it would make her wise. God's instructions were that eating from the tree would result in her death. It is true that the first humans were not going to suffer a physical death from eating of the tree. God was referring to a spiritual death, and because of their disobedience, sin entered the Earth. Satan corrupted the truth and declared God a liar. He said that eating the fruit would not kill her, but it would make her become like God (Genesis 3:4). He tried to convince her that God was keeping something beneficial away from her and her husband, when in actuality, God was protecting them. Because Adam and Eve fell into temptation, they were banished from the Garden of Eden, and now sin plagues humanity.

Satan took one aspect of the truth and twisted it to get the outcome he wanted. As a result, Adam and Eve lost their innocence, and when there is a loss of innocence, suspicion and cynicism develops. This distrust leads to self-preservation, which we see manifest as God confronts them. Self-preservation is engrossed in a heightened self-awareness, with little to no regard for others. This mentality is encouraged by the media, politics, and society in general. This includes those who have an unhealthy opinion about themselves, whether that assessment is high or low. Arrogance and self-pity are symptoms of embellished self-awareness. Emotionally, these may be opposites of each other, but both produce ungodly results.

During the conversation between Satan and Eve, we find that he has convinced her that doing wrong was actually for her benefit. As Eve mulls this notion around in her head, she considers it an opportunity to give her wisdom. If we deliberate the lies of the enemy too long, we will convince ourselves that we are receiving something we truly are not. The Tree of Knowledge of Good and Evil was not called the tree of wisdom (Genesis 3:6). We receive distorted truth when we incline our ear to Satan. He deceives, and the longer we listen to him, the more persuasive he becomes. Adam and Eve did not have scripture to help combat temptation, but they did have God's truth to rely on. The Bible is our weapon of warfare, and we will not lose our battles as long as we operate with the power of the Holy Spirit (Ephesians 6:10-18).

During this conversation, Eve was weighing the possibility of losing her life, and Satan was anticipating this. He capitalized on this matter, and Eve took the bait. The moment we elect to sin is the moment we choose ourselves over God. Eve's only rationale for not disobeying God was to preserve her life. This is evident in her sole argument in Genesis 3. After Satan negates this and misrepresents the truth, Eve loses her belief. Our decisions and actions are attributes of what we consider to be true. The way we sin reveals what we do and do not believe. Initially, Eve believed that eating from the tree would result in her losing her life, but once that conviction was altered, her actions changed. If we do not have a firm foundation on what we believe, we will go through life confused and grappling with our faith when things are not going favorably. We will all experience perplexing moments, but this is a reminder to revisit our foundational principles when those times come. When we experience hardships, it is necessary recall why we chose to accept the Lordship of Christ. We must remember why we chose Him and build our faith on the one who is trustworthy.

When we miss the mark, our actions can fall into any or all of the following categories:

1. Sins against God
2. Sins against ourselves
3. Sins against others

We are called to love God, and love others as ourselves (Mark 12:30-31). When we love, it is the fulfillment of the law, and when the law is satisfied, sin does not exist. It is typical to evade wrongdoing because we fear the consequences. We may even contemplate the people we might be hurting because of our behavior. When we choose God, we are rejecting the world. If our resistance to sin is based off of a fear of consequences, we do not truly understand who God is. Yes, there are consequences for our actions, and yes, grace does abound, but if we truly love God, we will keep His commandments (1 John 5:3). First Corinthians 10:13 (NIV) reads,

"No temptation has overtaken you that is not common to man. God is faithful, and he will not let you be tempted beyond your ability, but with the temptation he will also provide the way of escape, that you may be able to endure it."

Every sin begins with a thought, and we must take every thought and make it obedient to Christ (2 Corinthians 10:5). In essence, when we start planning possible scenarios and outcomes in favor of the temptation, we are giving life to sin. The likelihood of falling into sin is high if we take the time to formulate ideas and weigh the pros and cons. The battle begins in the mind, but it can also be demolished there. If we can change our thoughts, then we can change our actions. Our fight against temptation must be based on the belief that we can overcome by the power of Christ who strengthens us (Philippians 4:13).

One of the issues that spiraled into an irrevocable mistake for Eve is that she tried to convince a liar of the truth. The Bible tells us to resist the devil and he will flee from us (James 4:7). The more we try to persuade him, the more we will become skeptical of the truth. He is a deceiver, and he tries to legitimize his deception. We overcome the deceiver with the truth of God's word. The longer we entertain the thoughts, the more susceptible we become to a fall. God always offers a way of escape, but we have to choose the escape route. Satan has influenced society in several ways, and the more we look to the world for answers, the farther we drift away from truth and righteousness.

The importance of accountability is riddled within this account. It is imperative to have people in our lives that are not only going to encourage and equip us with wisdom, but will also be candid with us when we walk in error. Eve was not present when God told Adam not to eat of the Tree of Knowledge of Good and Evil. Since Adam was given the command, he was the designated authority. From this we can see that even those in authority have the ability to sin. We often make the mistake of thinking that people in leadership positions are infallible, but it is human nature to stumble. Yes, it is disheartening to see strong men and women in the faith make sinful decisions, but we must remember that Jesus is the standard. He is the only one who is blameless and perfect in every way.

Even though Adam was the head of Eve, his position did not make him flawless. They were both wrong for their decisions, and both received consequences for their actions, but God confronted Adam first because he was the one who was given the directive. Adam placed the blame on Eve who then blamed the serpent, yet these accusations did not exempt anyone from punishment (Genesis 3:14-19).

As believers, we must examine ourselves, even if other parties are at fault. We cannot give pride an opportunity to grow in our lives by not taking responsibility for our own actions. Pride is what led to the fall of Lucifer and his eternal banishment from heaven. He, who was once the minstrel of heaven, orchestrating wonderful praises that reverenced the LORD, is now known as Satan the deceiver and the accuser. His fate is sealed so tightly in condemnation that he will forever be known by the actions that caused his ruin. Let us serve the LORD with all of our heart and escape devastation.

The Law and the Promise

"For if those who depend on the law are heirs, faith means nothing and the promise is worthless, because the law brings wrath. And where there is no law there is no transgression." -Romans 4:14-15 (NIV)

The law was established to show us what sin is, and if we didn't have the law, we wouldn't know that we need God. After Christ, the purpose of the law is to show us our necessity for a forgiving God (Romans 3:20). There is a distinct difference between observing the law and fulfilling the law. The Mosaic laws were put into place so that humans could know the standards of the LORD. To appease the wrath of God, sacrifices and offerings had to be made to bring God's people back into His grace. With over 600 laws that the people of God had to abide by, it was impossible to meet the standard. The law failed to make us right with God, which is why He sent Christ. Jesus came to fulfill the requirements of God's law, and by grace through faith we are saved (Ephesians 2:8-9).

We must understand that Paul was not telling us to stop abiding by rules. He was clarifying that keeping the Law of Moses is the equivalent of rejecting Jesus as the atonement for our sins. Those who were choosing to abide by the Law were, in essence, revealing that they did not need Christ. Any good we accomplish will never be good enough. If we choose to use our works as a means of our salvation, we will find ourselves in a battle of wills:

- Observing the law vs. The fulfillment of the law
- Our humanly 'just' acts vs. The righteousness of Christ
- Perpetual battle vs. Everlasting victory
- I'm doing vs. It is done
- Attempting to please God vs. This is my Son, in whom I am well pleased

We must believe in a power that is greater than our own if we desire to experience the fullness of God's presence. Jesus Christ abolished the law and its regulations in His death, and fulfilled the law with His resurrection. He gives us the desire to do what pleases Him by the power of the Holy Spirit. Jesus explained the greatest commandments in Matthew 22:36-40 as loving God above all else, and then loving others as we love ourselves. In Matthew 5, Jesus instructed that even if you speak disdainfully about another person, or think about someone lustfully, you have committed sin. What a stark contrast to the laws of the

Old Testament (Exodus 21:24)! Where people focus on actions, God looks at the heart (Jeremiah 17:10).

It is appalling to hear about prominent leaders committing lewd acts that dishonor their name and the position they held because we expect them to consistently uphold themselves with nobility. We tend to believe that once someone reaches a certain platform, they should never engage in any exploits that would defame them and the community they serve. Nevertheless, Jesus Christ is the standard. We will always fall short in comparison to His perfection. We must remember that we are not Jesus—we are people striving to be like Him, and need His forgiveness when we miss the mark.

Being a good person isn't impactful, that is what we should do, but being a righteous person distinguishes us, and this can only be achieved by accessing a power that we cannot produce ourselves. The Holy Spirit makes it possible to live without sin because it is His power prompting us to walk in love. He graces us with power that surpasses our capabilities. Because of human frailty, we are inclined to sin, but the Holy Spirit can keep us from a life of sinfulness (Romans 8:9-14). There has to be a desire and belief in order to receive this power, and to understand this power, we must identify where it comes from.

Holy Spirit

The Holy Spirit is part of the Trinity—which is confirmed throughout scripture. In Hebrew, His name is 'ruach' and 'pneuma' which are literally translated as 'wind' and 'breath.' He is described in the New Testament as "Parakletos" which means Advocate and Helper.[4] The first mention of His presence is in Genesis 1:2, where He is hovering over the dark waters. In Genesis 1:26 (NIV) God said,

"Let us make mankind in our image, in our likeness..."

John 4:24 (NIV) declares,

"God is spirit, and his worshipers must worship in the Spirit and in truth."

God the Father, God the Son, and God the Holy Spirit make up the Triune God, which is God in three persons. The word 'Triune' denotes three in unity. Some may confuse this with polytheism, which is the worship of many gods, but Christianity is a monotheistic faith, specifying that we serve one God. We believe that He is

---

[4] Merrill C. Tenney, ed. *Zondervan's Pictorial Bible* (Grand Rapids: Zondervan, 1967), 358.

the only real, living, and true God, yet we are faced with the weighty topic of 'God in three persons.' This portion of the text intends to substantiate that the Holy Spirit is God.

The presence of the Holy Spirit can be seen throughout the Bible, and His manifestation and power are undeniable in the New Testament. In Matthew 3:16 and Luke 3:22 we read that the Holy Spirit came upon Jesus after His baptism. Soon after, Jesus was led into the wilderness to be tested. After successfully resisting the devil, Jesus began His ministry.

Scripture warns us that the unpardonable sin is blasphemy against the Holy Spirit (Matthew 12:32). This sin has been described as an unruly or hostile attitude. This is not as simple as saying something bad against the Holy Spirit, but it is an enduring attitude of disbelief that actively speaks against Him. If we are born again believers, we receive the Holy Spirit and He guides our lives. Blasphemy against the Spirit and not believing in God are synonymous. As previously stated, God does not send human beings to hell. On the contrary, it is the rejection of Jesus that prevents entrance into heaven. The same is true of the Holy Spirit.

If one does not accept Christ, this person inevitably does not have the Holy Spirit because he or she chooses not to believe in Him. Jesus told His disciples that He had to go so that He could send the 'Helper.' Prior to the death and resurrection of Christ, the Holy Spirit only came upon people to demonstrate His power. Without regard to role, position, or lineage, the Holy Spirit is now accessible to everyone who chooses Jesus as their LORD and Savior. It is by the Holy Spirit that we become capable of righteous living.

The Holy Spirit is our alternative to an unholy lifestyle. Ephesians 5:18 warns us against indulging in sinful pleasures, and it is because of the Holy Spirit that we are able to resist. Before we accept Christ into our hearts, it is in our nature to be devoted to ourselves. This egotistical inclination may look different from one person to the other, but the motivation is self-gratification. In this state we are in the bondage to sin. A slave does only as he is told, and has no freedom to do otherwise. After Christ, we receive the gift of righteousness, and the assurance that we are in right standing with God. We are no longer slaves to sin, and Romans 6 illustrates for us the difference between living for self and living for God.

Paul explains that before Christ enters our lives, we were slaves to our sinful nature. A great exchange takes place when we accept Christ—our sinfulness is replaced with righteousness. This virtue gives us right standing with God, despite being His enemies prior to salvation. Even while we were His enemies, Christ died for us (Romans 5:6-8). After salvation, we are no longer enemies of God, and the penalty for our sin is paid in full. Because of the Father's grace and mercy, we receive very precious parts of Him—His Son and His Spirit.

Throughout the Bible and history, there are countless stories of miracles and phenomena that man cannot explain with logic. Spiritual matters will always supersede human intellect. God deserves the glory because only He can release the miraculous. The same is true about the death and resurrection of Christ. The event surpasses human logic, which some have referred to as foolishness, and refuse to believe in a dying Savior. It does not make sense for a man to die for the sins of the world for a plethora of reasons.

First, who would choose to die for a people that rejected Him and deny His deity? Why would anyone choose to be convicted of a crime that he did not commit? How in the world does someone come back from the dead?

How is it possible for a baby to be incarnate? God's Word tells us that these things are not only true, but we are redeemed if we believe. The realities of God may seem foolish to the world, but we are wise for believing them (1 Corinthians 1:13-31).

It was by the power of the Holy Spirit that Jesus was able to begin His ministry. The Holy Spirit empowered Christ to do what He had not done before. The same is true for every believer. Once we are saved, the Holy Spirit begins His work in us as we submit to His will. He enables us to be who we have never been before, to do what we have never done before. For this to occur, we must understand that upon receiving Christ as LORD and Savior, we are filled with the Holy Spirit. This indwelling is the assurance of our salvation (Romans 8:16), making us confident that we have been redeemed through Christ. The role of the Holy Spirit is 'The Helper'. He is the reason why we have the ability to do what pleases God. In receiving His Spirit, we have obtained the ability to mature spiritually. Despite our flaws, God applies His love and grace, to grow, discipline, and encourage us to make us more like Him.

Before receiving the Holy Spirit, the best we could ever be is a self-righteous person. Living self-righteously signifies that Christ died for nothing (Galatians 2:21). Piety is a posture that conveys we will make ourselves good by controlling our behaviors. The reconciliation we receive through the death of Christ is the only deed that will ever make us 'good enough' for God. There is much danger in self-sufficiency. Often times this breeds apathy for the shortcomings of others and an astute attitude against those who appear weak-willed. This prideful mindset is an overemphasis of one's own goodness and an amplification of personal moral character. It is unhealthy and creates spaces for intolerance, and will soon demonstrate that we do not possess the attributes of a Christ follower. Pride is a spiritual sickness that leads to sin, and all of us are susceptible to it. Throughout scripture we are admonished of its symptoms and its likelihood of destruction. Proverbs 16:18 (ESV) warns,

"Pride goes before destruction, a haughty spirit before a fall."

Pride is a human frailty, though we find in Exodus 4:4-5 that God calls Himself a jealous God. One might question, if pride is sin, how can God be jealous? In context, this term in Exodus can only be applied to God and His desire for His creation to have an unwavering commitment to Him. His jealousy is a longing for His creation, and it breaks His heart when we prefer what is created over the Creator. The Father has a divine right to require our devotion. His jealousy will never lead Him to do wrong, unlike us as imperfect vessels. God, in all of His righteousness, can only bring about righteousness. Everything that He does is holy and zealous, which is a righteous passion and dedication. God could never be associated with the pride that results in arrogance and haughtiness.

In second Corinthians, Paul described the pain of the thorn in his side. He asked God to remove it three times, but it remained. Paul was receiving such powerful revelations that if God removed the thorn, Paul would have become haughty. He was not maliciously hurting Paul, but it was with the loving discipline of the Father that kept Paul's focus on Christ. The same concept is true for us. We may be experiencing thorns in our lives as well, and this discomfort is a catalyst to grow and prune us. It may seem cruel, but Proverbs 3:12 communicates that just as an Earthly father disciplines and corrects his Earthly son, our heavenly Father will discipline and correct His children. It is for our benefit, and we must trust that despite the pain, it will mold us into vessels that will become more like Christ. These experiences will incline our ears to His voice so that we become more cognizant of His plan for our lives. How can we accomplish this? Second Corinthians 10:5 (NIV) gives a wonderful tool:

"We demolish arguments and every pretension that sets itself up against the knowledge of God, and we take captive every thought to make it obedient to Christ."

Pride is an exaggerated view of one's capabilities or lack thereof. The problem arises when we set these conceptions of ourselves against what we know about God. If we understood Him well enough in the context of which we were falling, we would not choose to sin. For example, if we believe that God will provide a mate, we will not settle for someone we know is not God's best for us. If we believe that God makes us victorious, we wouldn't allow fear to discourage us from pursuing our dreams when things get difficult. If we have the assurance of God's grace, and are confident in the hope that He fills us with, we won't fall into temptation. To take it further, if we really knew God, we would never set an ideal up against the knowledge that we have about Him. When we continue to walk in sin, we are behaving in a manner that reveals that we do not know God (1 John 3:4-6).

When we are full of pride, we believe we are better than we really are. The opposite of pride is humility, and humility results in obedience. It can be very difficult to determine when we have allowed pride to govern our lives. We must question our motives and reflect on our actions and words. If we are seeking approval and fame, we can be certain that we are in the pursuit of our own glory. If we are living lives that illuminate the Father, we will not have to purposefully place ourselves in the limelight. If we magnify God, others will see the good He has placed inside of us. How can we identify pride in our lives? It is not as simple as one may think, especially when it is often easier to notice it in someone else before we ever perceive it in ourselves. Matthew 7:3-4 (NIV) asserts,

> *"Why do you look at the speck of sawdust in your brother's eye and pay no attention to the plank in your own eye? How can you say to your brother, 'Let me take the speck out of your eye,' when all the time there is a plank in your own eye?"*

These verses inform us that if we fail to assess ourselves, then we are worse off than those we are scrutinizing. That is why the fault within us (a plank) is juxtaposed with something so tiny (a speck). We have to be more willing to critique and repair ourselves than we are to execute the process for others. This self-examination brings an awakening unlike anything else. The enlightenment leads to humility, and our humility will guide us in our hope. When we exalt the Father, He will lift us up in honor (1 Peter 5:6).

Some use Matthew 7:3-4 as a means of advocating non-judgment or correction, but verse five clearly dissipates that theory:

"You hypocrite, first take the plank out of your own eye, and then you will see clearly to remove the speck from your brother's eye." (NIV)

Many times the error spoken of in this verse is the result of pride. It is not uncommon for us to see a flaw in someone else and think we are better off because we do not have to deal with that particular issue. Any time we elevate ourselves in this manner we have uncovered a symptom of pride. Pride is especially dangerous because if it is not checked, it has the potential to cause many sins. Proverbs 29:23 (NIV) teaches the following:

"Pride ends in humiliation, while humility brings honor."

Throughout the Bible we are warned against haughtiness. This is an indication that it happens more often than we realize or would like to admit. It increases the likelihood of self-deception, which is exceptionally dangerous because it produces the belief that we are right when we are actually wrong. This is a place of spiritual darkness and makes the person susceptible to other attacks and tricks of the enemy. To avoid this, it would be best for us to examine ourselves often and ask God to search our hearts. Psalm 19:12-13 (NLT) imparts,

"How can I know all the sins lurking in my heart? Cleanse me from these hidden faults. Keep your servant from deliberate sins! Don't let them control me. Then I will be free of guilt and innocent of great sin."

In Matthew 7, Jesus is not telling us that we cannot identify sin in someone else. He is instructing us to conduct a self-assessment and question our own motives: Why are we so interested in what they are doing? Is our goal accountability? Are we seeking to help them improve their Christian walk? Has God led us to confront the sin? Are we open to the same accountability? If we are operating in the right spirit, it is our responsibility to hold each other accountable the way He has prescribed in His word. If this were not true, Jesus would not have said we would be able to remove the speck from another's eye. He admonishes us to first take the plank out of our own eye before approaching the speck in someone else's eye

(Matthew 7:5). There are other passages of scripture that depict accountability among believers. Galatians 6:1-2 (NIV) reveals,

"Brothers and sisters, if someone is caught in a sin, you who live by the Spirit should restore that person gently. But watch yourselves, or you also may be tempted. Carry each other's burdens, and in this way you will fulfill the law of Christ."

We can check ourselves by examining our motives and our emotions. It is imperative to know who we are, and what our intentions are with those around us. What is the lasting expectation? If that outcome does not glorify God, and does not leave everyone involved better than they were before, we can be sure that pride is the superimposing factor. Accountability will be discussed in more detail in the next section.

God desires for us to be prolific and to accomplish marvelous feats for the Kingdom. In John 15, Jesus tells us that He is the vine, we are the branches, and God the Father is the gardener. A gardener is responsible for the upkeep of the garden. There is a lot of work involved in the maintenance. First, we see that branches that do not produce fruit are cut off. This is not a reference to the world, but to those who have accepted Him as Savior.

What good are we in the kingdom of God if we do nothing to expand it?

While unproductive branches are cut off, the branches that produce fruit are pruned. The term 'prune' describes a trimming process that is used to cleanse the branches to make them more fruitful. In a spiritual sense, God wants to sever the things in us that are unfruitful. This, of course, can only occur with our cooperation. If we choose not to be fruitful, we will be cut off from the tree. If we desire to be fruitful, then we desire the will of God. He is the mastermind and knows exactly what must be done for us to perform at our best. We may not always enjoy the process, but there is an incomparable satisfaction that comes when we fulfill our purpose.

Paul explained in Romans 4 that no one can earn righteousness, but it is accredited to us by faith. He clarified this revelation by equating it to working for payment. When we go to work, we expect compensation, and we should be compensated, if that was the agreement between the employer and the employee. Most of us work in order to obtain something. When it comes to salvation and right standing with God, we only obtain it by what we believe (Romans 4:5).

"If God's promise is only for those who obey the law, then faith is not necessary and the promise is pointless." -Romans 4:14 (NLT)

It is not by obeying the law that gets us in right standing with God, it is by our faith in Jesus Christ that allows our sins to be forgiven, and it is through Him that we gain access into heaven. It is based on what He did, not what we do because salvation is a gift. We cannot earn it and there is nothing that we could ever do to deserve it. Because we love Him, we obey His commands. We don't obey His commands because we want Him to love us; He loved us while we were still His enemies! We can live every day doing great things, but if we never believe in Jesus, we will never make it through heaven's gates.

On multiple occasions we will fail to meet the standard of perfection, which is Christ. The veil was torn when Jesus died (Matthew 27:51). This was symbolic for the barrier between us and God being removed forever. He dismantled the need for a human mediator and gave us direct access to the kingdom of God. We no longer need a priest to make atonement for our sins, because our intercessor is Jesus Christ. The Holy Spirit teaches us what to pray, and utters the words we may not know to say on our behalf (Romans 8:26-27). The power and wisdom of the Holy Spirit are infinite, and we could never function accordingly without Him. He is the conductor of our faith.

A conductor makes it possible for power to travel. Before we have right standing with God, it is impossible to know Him and do what is pleasing to Him. With the Holy Spirit, we are given the immense potential to walk in godliness.

Hope in the Struggle

We can be certain that the God we serve is not a God who is far off. Some believe that God puts things into motion and allows us to decide how to function without His assistance or watchfulness. There are many different beliefs about God and the range of conviction varies tremendously from person to person. What we can be sure of is our entire universe was formulated by the most incredible mind that ever existed. He knew us before conception and He has an astonishing plan for every person on this planet.

As our loving Father, He walks with us through our hardships and misfortunes. Long ago, He suffered for us, and if we suffer, we know that we belong to Him (Romans 8:17). First Peter 4 explains that just as Christ suffered, we, too, would experience suffering. A life in Christ does not guarantee of a life free of difficulties. It would be a disappointing existence to believe that our lives are supposed to be free of any and all pain. This isn't the case even for those who do not know Christ! Unfortunately, this thought becomes very common, and when the struggles of life arise, some reject their faith.

There are some who live in the lap of luxury, while others struggle, and others are poor. Some people are celebrities, some have an amount of prestige, and others lead common lives. God does not choose us based on what we do or not have. We are chosen to be His people in spite of the frailties of this world and the inadequacies within ourselves. The only expectation God has for us is submission under His divine authority. Not only should we submit to Him, but we must also submit to the leadership that is over us, such as supervisors and officials. We may disagree with their directives for various reasons, but Romans 13:1-7 substantiates the importance of us following the authority governing us despite our thoughts and feelings towards them. If the Son of God surrendered when He had the power to eradicate His accusers, we too, are called to a life of submission.

"So then, since Christ suffered physical pain, you must arm yourselves with the same attitude he had, and be ready to suffer, too. For if you have suffered physically for Christ, you have finished with sin. You won't spend the rest of your lives chasing your own desires, but you will be anxious to do the will of God." -1Peter 4:1-2 (NLT)

Suffering is not exclusive to things such as death, sickness, or tragedies of this magnitude. We also experience pain when we resist things that our flesh craves. In this scripture, we see that we will suffer when we are refraining from doing what is appealing to us so that we may please the LORD. When we value His will more than our own, we will do the opposite of what pleases the flesh. This could mean giving up an activity that once brought us a lot of satisfaction, completing tasks we've never done before, or embracing the unfamiliar. At times it may seem as though we are putting ourselves in the face of danger for the sake of the cross, but giving our lives to Him is the least we could do for the one who laid down His life for us.

With the knowledge we have about Jesus, we should understand that we do not serve a God who does not know pain. He suffered on the cross, and He suffers with us in our distress. While on the cross he felt the weight of the world. He took past, present, and future sins upon Himself and died to rescue a perishing world. He lived on Earth and experienced human emotions. Jesus knows how it feels to love (John 19:26), to empathize (John 11:33), to wait (Luke 3:23), to be timid (John 2:4-5), to struggle (Luke 22:24), to suffer (Matthew 27), and to be wronged (Luke 22:48). Any emotion we have ever felt, Jesus had the privilege of facing. He is a God who knows us and cares for us, and according to Romans 8:17 (NIV), if we suffer for Jesus, we know that we will also reign with Him as co-heirs.

"Now if we are children, then we are heirs—heirs of God and co-heirs with Christ, if indeed we share in his sufferings in order that we may also share in his glory."

Those of us in the faith are not necessarily called to a life of ease. We will endure trials, but He allows us to see glimmers of heaven while we live on Earth. We can find heaven in the devotion of family, the presence of friends, the accolades of accomplishments, the natural beauty of the Earth, and the list continues. The reprehensible circumstances of our lives make us appreciate and cherish the admirable experiences that we are blessed with.

In the latter part of Matthew 16, Jesus prophesies about His trial and death. Despite knowing He would suffer a horrendous death, Jesus persisted in accomplishing the will of the LORD. He could have disbanded Judas, averted the arrest, and taken Himself off of the cross. As the Son of God, He could have done a myriad of things to comfort Himself. Jesus had the power not to die, but chose to die because He desired the Father's will more than preserving His life.

After Jesus addressed the disciples, Peter pulls Him to the side and rebukes Him for His words (Matthew 16:22). It was unbearable for Peter to hear that Christ would suffer such a travesty. Moreover, Peter wanted Jesus to stay with them for as long as possible. Peter was speaking of his own comforts with no regard for the will of God. This is evident in Jesus' rebuke, expressing that Peter did not have the concerns of God on his mind. Peter's concern was to have Jesus with him. God's concern was to give Jesus to the world. After rebuking Peter, Jesus admonished the disciples to take up their crosses and walk.

If we want to be like Jesus, we must abandon our own comforts. He modeled this for us by satisfying the will of the Father. On the brink of death, and after enduring false accusations, Jesus relinquished His life to fulfill the plan of God. The everlasting pleasures of heaven are unrivaled by everything on this Earth. Our need for heaven trumps every Earthly desire we will ever have. Therefore, the momentary afflictions we endure cannot be compared to the glory of His kingdom (2 Corinthians 4:17).

What good comes from building our castles on Earth only to enjoy it for a lifetime? The extent of our enjoyment after toiling to obtain things in this life is fleeting. With this in mind, we must be farsighted, holding onto the things that are to come. Throughout the New Testament, we find that our final and lasting hope is eternity in heaven. This hope should outlast any other Earthly hope in our minds, and should be the greatest desire in our hearts. As long as we live, there will always be a need for another blessing. Heaven is perfection, and we will lack no good thing in eternity. This may be very difficult to comprehend when the very nature inside of us craves immediacy. It is innate to focus on the now when later seems so far away. It is challenging because we would like to experience pleasures while on Earth, and we will, but God promises us so much more than that. Romans 8:18 (NLT) imparts,

"Yet what we suffer now is nothing compared to the glory he will reveal to us later."

This 'later' could indicate any number of time frames, but ultimately we are waiting for the day of redemption. The glorious freedom from death and decay is eternal life with Christ in heaven. The verses in Romans 8 instruct us that the Holy Spirit is a preview of this glory. It is the evidence of Him in our lives that is our everlasting blessing. He gives us power that only comes from heaven, and equips us to experience the essence of God while on

Earth. When we receive blessings, we know that we receive because of Him. He unlocks doorways and exposes pathways that would have never been available to us without Him. More than anything, the Holy Spirit is the indication and the assurance of what we will receive. For further clarification, this passage is not suggesting that God won't give us the desires of our heart, but it is a reminder that there is something even more glorious than the things we ask for in this life. There is no doubt that we will experience incredible victories in Christ, but the presence of sin and suffering will remain as long as we live on this Earth. When God reveals who His children are (those of us who have accepted His Son as LORD) we will be liberated from the demise of mankind forever. God not only promises to deliver us in this life, but He will set us free permanently in the life that is to come.

As recorded in Matthew 17, Jesus and three of His disciples went to the mountain top where His transfiguration took place. There was vibrancy of light, and He was seen standing with Moses and Elijah. For the disciples, this was confirmation that Jesus was the Messiah. After this experience, Peter suggests building a memorial for Jesus, and, as chronicled in verse five, they hear the voice of God saying,

"This is my Son, whom I love; with him I am well pleased. Listen to him!" (NIV)

Jesus does not concede to Peter's proposal of being memorialized, and this isn't the only occurrence. When Jesus fed five thousand in John 6:16, His royalty was presumed. Those in attendance recognized His amazing power and wanted to appoint Him as king. When Jesus perceived this, He went away to be alone. While on Earth, Jesus's view was set on the Kingdom of God. He had several opportunities to be king while on the Earth, but He understood the ultimate promise was to be King of Eternity.

Jesus was aware of the things He would suffer, and even pleaded with God to take it away from Him, yet He still chose to obey and do the will of the Father. For His obedience, He is the God of our salvation who can never be defeated! He is coming back for His bride, which is the church, and promises to do away with every evil and wicked thing that has ever attempted to overrule and overpower mankind. He loved us more than His own life, and suffered because of His obedience. We know that Jesus took on human nature and became like us. He felt the same emotions we feel, and most likely desired the same things we do. Many of us like to be recognized and acknowledged for our good deeds. Yet, we see that even Jesus had to deny Himself the opportunity to be revered, and suffered for His decision for God. He instructs us to take on the same attitude, which is recorded in Matthew 16:24 (NLT):

"If any of you wants to be my follower, you must turn from your selfish ways, take up your cross, and follow me."

Our individual crosses may contrast significantly, but each cross bestows affliction in some capacity. Yet, with hope and expectation, we patiently endure knowing that we have the victory.

Almost everything that we do presents us with some sort of delay. These moments of character building are meant to produce patience. Things as simple as standing in line, commuting to and from work, doing laundry, and even preparing food require a certain measure of patience. Then there are the more cumbersome things such as marriage, the birth of a child, or saving money to purchase a car or a home. One thing all believers are expecting to see is the return of Christ. If Jesus has yet to come nearly 2,000 years later, and He said while He was absent He would be preparing a place for us (John 14:2), it must be the most extravagant and elaborate set up that we couldn't even begin to fathom.

Nevertheless, the treasures of this world make it difficult to focus on what we cannot see. We can be confident knowing that the things of this world will pass away, while the things of God will last forever. According to 1 John 2:15-17, the world will make us crave worldly things. If we become too engrossed in it, we will start to desire things more than God. There is nothing wrong with enjoying possessions, but if our desire for treasure is causing rifts in our relationship with Christ, we must evaluate ourselves.

With the assurance of Christ, we eagerly await the promises of God, but how do we wait? What is our countenance? What do we do in the meantime? How does this wait time increase our patience? Are we maximizing opportunities to grow and reflect in these moments? Are we using these opportunities for spiritual growth? At times it may seem that even minor things can frustrate us and bigger obstructions may even cause us to lose hope. Yet we have a hope that does not fail. Jeremiah 17:7-9 (NIV) imparts,

"But blessed is the one who trusts in the LORD, whose confidence is in him. They will be like a tree planted by the water that sends out its roots by the stream. It does not fear when heat comes; its leaves are always green. It has no worries in a year of drought and never fails to bear fruit."

If we continue to trust and believe in the one who is trustworthy, we will not be put to shame (Romans 10:11). We endure these moments of long suffering with the expectation that it will get better. We believe that one day every obstacle, complication, pain, sickness, and evil that we have suffered will be done away with forever. Though we wait for promises, we live for the promise, and all of God's promises lead to Christ.

When we speak of the law, we must also affirm the promise, which is Christ. Everything that ever was, and everything that ever will be was created by Him and for Him. It is because of Him that all things are able to function and work for our good. Jesus is the epitome of the promise that we anticipate, and one day He will bring us into His now (Colossians 1:15-20).

"For no matter how many promises God has made, they are "Yes" in Christ. And so through him the "Amen" is spoken by us to the glory of God." -2 Corinthians 1:20 (NIV)

Before we were born, and before the formation of the Earth, God had an amazing plan and purpose for each and every individual on the planet. He intricately designed and fashioned all of us for a specific and divine moment in time. He often communicates these plans to us, and equips us to fulfill them, but, we frequently find ourselves waiting for the fruition of what we hope for. This scripture tells us that if God spoke it, it will happen. We exercise our faith by saying, "and it is so!" His 'yes' indicates a covenant with us and a promise to satisfy it. Our 'amen' acknowledges the faithfulness of the promise, and an eager expectation for its completion. Whenever it seems like the promise will not be fulfilled, we must remind ourselves that 'it is so!' This is speaking presently about something that will happen in the future. We must believe that it is not only going to happen, but is happening now!

Living for Christ can be one of the most challenging decisions of our lives, but it is also the most rewarding. There is no greater incentive than to have the most loving, and most powerful being on our side. When the world comes up against us, He fights on our behalf. Even when we are our own worst enemy, He positions us for victory by the power of His Holy Spirit. Despite the pain and suffering we endure, we know that we have a God who suffers with us. He does not cause our suffering, but when we trust the plan that He has for us, He orchestrates our victory and brings out the best in us. In addition to this, God entrusts us with very precious parts of Himself—His Son and His Spirit.

The Holy Spirit is our comforter and counselor. He instructs us in the ways that we should go, and gives us the ability to accomplish things we could have never done apart from Him. Though we have hope in this life, we have an eternal hope in the life that is to come. When situations and circumstances come against us, Jesus is our final answer. When we depend on Him, He rages war against our enemy and gives us victory over the kingdom of darkness. Our hope will outlast our doubts if we continually visualize our triumph before it manifests. It is not by our own strength, but by the power that comes from the Most High God (Zechariah 4:6).

But he said to me, "My grace is sufficient for you, for my power is made perfect in weakness." Therefore I will boast all the more gladly about my weaknesses, so that Christ's power may rest on me. That is why, for Christ's sake, I delight in weaknesses, in insults, in hardships, in persecutions, in difficulties. For when I am weak, then I am strong.

2 Corinthians 12:9-10 (NIV)

Part III

Love

"And now these three remain: faith, hope and love. But the greatest of these is love." ~1 Corinthians 13:13 (NIV)

Love Adoration

There are principles of love that we are very familiar with—the bond of lovers, the protection of a parent, the companionship of a pet, the camaraderie of a friend, the fondness of food, or the excitement of an activity. With any of these, we marvel at the peak of enjoyment, and agonize at the depth of sorrow. We love hard, yet many are not taught that the highest and purest form of love is best understood after experiencing pain. It is not until we familiarize ourselves with polar opposites that we can truly apprehend the fulfillment of love. To those who depend on logic, this seems absurd, but as we have discussed, the application of faith is not meant to be understood, but radically exercised. When we are faced with the unknown, we must resolve to take the leap into the mysterious, uncomfortable, or unfamiliar. This leap of faith reveals our trust in the God that we cannot see.

This section is about the application of life, which is love. In love, we will find forgiveness, humility, and unity. Love is an often misunderstood thing, and perhaps we are never meant to understand it. Maybe we were created to exemplify it in its highest form—to love even when it hurts. Hebrews 5:8-10 (ESV) reads,

"Although he was a son, he learned obedience through what he suffered. And being made perfect, he became the source of eternal salvation to all who obey him, being designated by God a high priest after the order of Melchizedek."

Jesus learned obedience from the things that He suffered. With this knowledge there is an implication that Jesus had the power not to die on the cross. He is God! If He had the power to drive out demons, raise the dead, and heal the sick, there is no question that He had the power to take Himself off of the cross. This argument was used as a taunt against Him in Matthew 27:32-44. They understood that if He could perform miracles, then surely He could save Himself, yet He chose to subject Himself despite His authoritative stance. Our position as Christians is also a position of power because God has given us the wonderful gift of choice. That choice gives us the power to choose ordinary lives, or to live extraordinarily with the power of God infused within us.

This God-given freedom of choice allows us to love beyond reason. Life and death, and good and evil, all lie within the choices that we make. God gives all people the freedom to live however we see fit, but as our adoring admirer, His hope is that we would choose Him. The

Creator knows what He intended to accomplish when He fashioned His creation (Isaiah 29:16).

The things we devote our time, attention, and affections to confirm what we love. Our focus may be on wealth, family, ministry, or relationships, and all of these things are acceptable within reason, but as believers, we must love God above all else. The depiction of the crucifixion is proof enough that Jesus loves us. He gave up His rights as royalty, and His dignity as a man, to demonstrate the true meaning of love. When we allow God to order our steps, our choices reflect the level of respect and care we have for Him. If we have made our own way despite heeding warnings from the Father, we are not utilizing our power of choice for good. How can we know the difference? When can we be sure that we are living for God?

"If we live by the Spirit, let us also keep in step with the Spirit. Let us not become conceited, provoking one another, envying one another." -Galatians 5:25-26 (ESV)

If our intentions and efforts are being driven by a desire to elevate self, we are robbing God of glory that only belongs to Him. Our lives should always point to the one we are living for. This does not mean we will never be recognized (though many believers can attest to being overlooked), but our intention should be to elevate Christ in all that we do. To put it simply, we must lose control of our own agendas. Colossians 3:4 (ESV) teaches us that,

"When Christ who is your life appears, then you also will appear with him in glory."

When we live for Christ in a way that abandons our comforts, there is an incomprehensible glory that not only elevates God but propels us to another level in Him. Our trust and steadfastness demonstrate to the world that there is someone greater who desires to be known in tremendous ways. He desires to share those moments of glory with us. In Romans 8:17 we find that we are joint heirs with Christ. When we suffer for the sake of Christ, we will also experience His glory. When we testify and share our battles and victories with others, His glory is revealed through us. Our suffering is temporary, but in the end we will possess an eternal blessing.

First Corinthians 13 gives us descriptions of what love is, and what it is not. Paul eloquently conveys that even if we accomplish marvelous works for the Kingdom, it would be nothing if we do not walk in love. He speaks of things that we value in the church, such as prophecy and knowledge, but instructs us that without love, it means nothing. So what is love? Verses 4-8, reveal that,

> *"Love is patient, love is kind. It does not envy, it does not boast, it is not proud. It does not dishonor others, it is not self-seeking, it is not easily angered, it keeps no record of wrongs. Love does not delight in evil but rejoices with the truth. It always protects, always trusts, always hopes, always perseveres. Love never fails..." (NIV)*

Love exemplifies what we are not on our own. It is much easier to be impatient, unpleasant, envious, arrogant, and selfish. We already know what we want, and it is typically easier for us to look out for ourselves rather than someone else. It is true that we should love ourselves, but we should love others as much as we love ourselves (Mark 12:31).

Loving others does not mean disregarding ourselves, but rather it is a courtesy we give to others that we would want for ourselves. Many of us were taught to treat others the way we want to be treated, and even non-Christian principles adhere to the Golden Rule in Matthew 7:12 (ESV),

> *"So whatever you wish that others would do to you, do also to them, for this is the Law and the Prophets."*

Scripture tells us that love is the fulfillment of the law because it does no wrong to its neighbor (Galatians 5:14; Romans 13:10). If we love ourselves, then we know how to love others. This task cannot be done with human ingenuity alone. It takes divine intervention from heaven to empower us to love unconditionally.

If we want to operate in the purest form of love, we must lose our desire to be in control. This is how God shows His love for us by giving humanity free will. When we love, we are not seeking to control everything that someone else does. We give the other party an opportunity to develop and express who they are, instead of imposing who we want them to be. If we are being patient with someone, we are no longer trying to get them to do what we want them to do, when we want them to do it. We are also not trying to stipulate how they perform. This love offers grace when we would rather give wrath. It involves giving an opportunity for someone else to pursue a goal without criticizing them or holding offense against them. Even when we think we are being treated unfairly, we do the right thing anyway. Love is displaying goodness without publicizing it. Love does not perpetually remind others of their faults.

"Jesus replied, "you must love the LORD your God with all your heart, all your soul, and all your mind.' This is the first and greatest commandment. The second is equally important: 'Love your neighbor as yourself.' The entire law and all the demands of the prophets are based on these two commandments." -Matthew 22:37-40 (NLT)

We are to love God, and love others as we love ourselves. What we find is that love is putting others on the same level as ourselves, but placing God above all. In practice, we show the same consideration that we would want for ourselves, even if it is not reciprocated. However, if we are not careful about tending to this dynamic, it will become unbalanced. Sin is accredited to our free will, but it is free will that causes our acts of love to be so powerful. God's love for humanity meant granting His creation the freedom to choose Him, even though He could have forced us to serve Him. With this gift of free will, God has given us the power to fall madly in love with Him and to tragically break His heart.

Love is a lifestyle, and by definition, a lifestyle is how we live. We understand that before all else, we live for God, and then we live for others as we live for ourselves. While the world glorifies hedonism, it is what we do for others that will bring glory to God. The ways of the world will always resist godliness. Romans chapter twelve reminds us that we should not follow the patterns of this world. Even though it is not in our nature to love the way the Bible instructs us to, the Holy Spirit guides us in this lifestyle. His magnificent power and grace enable us to exude love at the Kingdom level.

It is very common to believe that we are to love others more than ourselves, but that is not what scripture tells us. We must find the healthy balance of meeting the needs of others as we take care of our own, though at times it may mean that we go without some things. However, this does not mean that we completely neglect our own health and wellness. We must be prayerful about the sacrifices we make for others and use wisdom in regards to how to demonstrate love. If we do not take care of ourselves, we won't be able to take care of anyone else.

The ways we show love for others demonstrates how we love ourselves, even if it seems like we are suffering in that moment. For example, if there is a family member or co-worker who annoys us without much effort, it does not show the love of God to tell them everything we do not like about them. Showing the love of God means exhibiting patience and restraint by refraining from reacting in an ungodly way. It may mean giving an item to someone else that you really wanted for yourself, or being the first to apologize in a disagreement. Refusing to pacify the flesh can be painful, but it will never compare to the joy of blessing others. Suffering in this capacity is an indication of spiritual maturity, and this progression is a sign of obedience. Obedience always leads to death of the sinful nature and life to the spirit. The flesh opposes God, so when we walk in obedience, we can count it as joy that sin is losing its hold on us as we cling to godliness.

Obedience

Suffering is not always a consequence of sin or a wrong we have committed. Often, suffering can be an indication that there is something we must obtain before advancing to another level. The pain enables us to have the capacity to manage difficult things. It empowers us to relate and minister to others who are experiencing the same things we endured. This may be hard to understand because we are taught that God is a just and benevolent God who doesn't want to hurt us. This is true, but everything that is painful is not necessarily harmful. When we surrender our lives to Him, the parts of us that could potentially hurt others and ourselves are subjected to the authority of Christ. Submission is not a derogatory term. In fact, it is a position of power. Even Jesus had to learn this principle while He lived on Earth. Philippians 2:8 (NIV) states,

> *"And being found in appearance as a man, he humbled himself by becoming obedient to death—even death on a cross!"*

When Jesus humbled Himself, it allowed God the opportunity to elevate Him. The anguish Jesus endured refined Him, and transformed Him to be the Savior of the

Universe. His death led to Him possessing the most powerful name in the world! Our suffering matures us, allowing us to become what God intended for us to become since the beginning of time.

"For I know the plans I have for you," declares the LORD, "plans to prosper you and not to harm you, plans to give you hope and a future."
-Jeremiah 29:11 (NIV)

First Peter 5:10 assures us that our suffering is temporary. We can be certain that God Himself will strengthen us and enable us to overcome the enemy (1 Corinthians 15:57). During the trials of life, there are questions that we should ask ourselves:

- Even though we are suffering, are we willing to surrender to the will of God?
- What knowledge can we take from this experience?

The parable of the two sons found in Matthew 21:28-31 depicts a father going to one son and asking him to work in the vineyard. For whatever reason, the son says that he will not do it, but later changes his mind and does the work. Because of the initial answer of the first son, the father goes to the second son and asks him to do it. The second son agrees to do so, but never does. After relaying this parable,

Jesus asked His listeners who did the will of the father, and the listeners responded that the first son did.

In Matthew 26:41, Jesus found His disciples sleeping even though He asked them to pray. His reaction to this scene was a rebuke, and then He said that the spirit is willing, but the flesh is weak. Obedience is subjecting our flesh into compliance under the authority of the Holy Spirit. The difference between the two sons is that the first did not want to (flesh is weak), but later completed the task (spirit is willing). The other son said that he would (spirit is willing), but never did (flesh is weak). The first son responded first with his flesh, and then with his spirit, and in doing so, pleased his father. The second son responded with his spirit, but had no follow through with his actions, and therefore, did not produce fruit. God is more concerned about what we do rather than what we say. The Christian life is a life of action. God will ask us to do things that may not make any sense to us, yet He will still require submission.

"Remember, it is sin to know what you ought to do and then not to do it." -James 4:17 (NLT)

It is wrong for us to know the right thing to do and not do it. Furthermore, we must be willing to trust God despite our lack of understanding the purpose. Our love for the Father will result in obedience despite our feelings.

Pain can be an unpleasant teacher, yet it can also be the catalyst that primes us for our destinies. Working through our hurts with hope fashions us into holy people, and equips us to help others. While we are going through turmoil, it may seem unbearable. As believers, we know that it is His power and strength that makes us more than conquerors (Romans 8:37). Becoming a Christian does not exempt us from every hardship, but His grace abounds in our circumstances.

There may have been several instances in the past when we were spared and can attest to the dangers and penalties we could have experienced. The anguish we are not spared from works for our benefit (Romans 8:28). Once we apprehend our purpose, there is a sense of calm, tenacity, and dependence on God that overtakes us. Our aim in any battle is to gain perseverance, character, and hope (Romans 5:3-5). Any time we have hope it will not disappoint us (Psalm 25:3). In the midst of hope, we will be confronted with our doubts and reservations because of our experiences. We must put our trust in a God that we do not always understand, accepting that His ways are greater than our own.

Sometimes the length of a test is associated with our willingness, participation, and expectation. James 1:2-4 teaches us that when we are suffering it is an opportunity for great joy. If we find ourselves always being tested, then we should always have joy. Though our immediate reaction to any opposition is far from delightful, our joy should be ascribed to the fact that God loves us and is always on our side. If we know that God loves us then we should walk in the assurance that we have His favor, regardless of what we are contending with. If we love Him then we will surrender to Him and accomplish His will for our lives. This obedience will fill us with the joy of the LORD, which is our strength (Nehemiah 8:10). When we are confident that we have the favor of God, we rest assured knowing that we will spend all of eternity with Him.

If we gain nothing else but perseverance after a trial, we can be convinced that we have progressed tremendously. James 1:4 teaches us that when perseverance finishes its work, we lack nothing. Therefore, having expectations is part of the will of God, both in this life and the life to come. Perseverance reminds us that there is something far better than what we are currently experiencing. Despite the troubles of this world, we can take comfort in John 16:33 (NLT):

"I have told you all this so that you may have peace in me. Here on earth you will have many trials and sorrows. But take heart, because I have overcome the world."

Forgiveness

It is common for us to look back at something we have done and not feel very proud of that moment. We may marvel if we didn't get caught and occasionally feel the pang of guilt from the damage it caused. We can think back to adolescence for the moment when a parent or guardian was disappointed in us. In some cases the disappointment felt heavier than the consequence. It is natural to feel remorseful for the wrong that we do, but there is a difference between remorse and guilt. Guilt makes us believe things about ourselves that are contrary to the Word of God. Guilt also makes it easier for us to accept punishment rather than forgiveness.

Could this be why many cannot accept a dying Savior's proposition of salvation and forgiveness? Is it possible that we are more willing to accept what we deserve (death) rather than what we are offered (life)? When Jesus forgave us, He gave His life in advance, like a trust fund. A trust fund is a collection of resources a benefactor prepares for a beneficiary to have financial security. This trust fund is given to the beneficiary once they reach a certain age, or after a certain event occurs. Before it is received, there is a manager of the funds who can make provisions, but eventually, the trust fund and all of its entitlements will be given to the beneficiary. Jesus is our benefactor. He built our trust fund of salvation by conquering the grave and taking authority over the kingdom of darkness. He managed it with His death and resurrection. He extends allowances of His grace and mercy as our provision until the day we decide to give our lives to Him. It is in the moment of our unwavering dedication that we receive the most promising security heaven has to offer.

Forgiveness for us meant suffering, pain, and agony for Jesus. In exchange for our faults, guilt, and shame, He presents freedom, love, and life. To fulfill this exchange He died a gruesome death, and for a short period of time was separated from the one He loved the most. When we forgive others, we are extending the same freedom, love, and life for those who have hurt us. In Christ, we have the power to forgive sins. Pardoning others and ourselves does not negate that there was a fault, but we bear with the offender by extending mercy. Forgiveness is letting go of our right to injure. This pardoning allows the forgiver to release the offender from the offense. The moment we release people from the pain we incurred is the moment we realize that Satan is our real enemy. It is easy to be mad at people, but they are not our adversaries. Satan works to make sure this truth goes undetected.

When Jesus surrendered His life on the cross He was blameless. He did nothing wrong, but still allowed Himself to be murdered. In fact, He was ridiculed and abused, and still refrained from defending Himself. In His last moments on this Earth He faced all past, present, and future sins of the world. He chose to withstand a consequence He did not earn by choosing to love. The same is true when someone offends us. Forgiveness is the choice to acknowledge that a wrong has been committed, and in spite of it, give love when it is unwarranted. When we pardon an offense, we are walking in love. Often the pain from the transgression comes at no fault of our own, but rather the thoughtless, insensitive, and sometimes brutal actions of others. In spite of that, we are called to face these transgressions, and instead of retaliating, we show love by forgiving the way Jesus does.

In His death, burial, and resurrection, Jesus gave us the ability to forgive sins. Satan fights against every power that is given to us by the Holy Spirit to cause us to forfeit these gifts. This power to forgive sins also grants us the power of reconciliation. Second Corinthians 5:18 says that Jesus gave us the ministry of reconciliation, which is necessary for hostile beings. When we are seeking to reconcile, we are working to change, make otherwise, or contrary to what someone or something once was.[5] When we were of the world, it was impossible to do what pleased God because we were His enemies. Even still, God desired us and sent His Son to reconcile Himself to us. Jesus was without fault, and took the fault of all creation so that we could enjoy eternity with Him. When we repent, God's love washes over us and makes us whole. He loves us, and believes that we are so valuable, that it was necessary for Him to die.

If Jesus, who was tortured, beaten, and killed, can offer reconciliation to those that hated Him, how much more so should we be willing to offer it to those who have wounded us? If we take part in the ministry of reconciliation, the goal is to assist the offender to become the opposite of what they currently are. When we forgive, it may seem that the guilty party is escaping punishment, but the act of pardoning transforms both the forgiven and the forgiver. When we forgive we become more like Christ.

---

[5] James Strong, *Katallage. In The Strongest Strong's Exhaustive Concordance of the Bible.*
(Grand Rapids: Zondervan, 2001) 2643.

Jesus died to prove His love. Because He died, believers must die to the desires of the flesh by abstaining from its immoral cravings. This death to sin leads to a life of selflessness. When our lives have been transformed by God, we are given the ability to live for God. When we say we believe in Christ, our old ways die, and we are resurrected into a new life. This new life is one of righteousness, enabling us to do what pleases the Father. He exchanges our old life for a new one in Him, and sin loses its authority over us. Jesus died and was raised back to life and will never die again. If we have issues forgiving others, that behavior must die to Christ. If we were once susceptible to bitterness, malice and the like, these old customs are buried with the burial of Christ. What is raised up is a life of righteousness that only comes from Him.

"And he died for all, that those who live should no longer live for themselves but for him who died for them and was raised again." -2 Corinthians 5:15 (NIV)

This spiritual death changes the emotional and social aspects of our lives. Romans chapter six conveys that Jesus died once and now lives in God. After we die to the flesh and ungodly lifestyles, we are joined with Christ. Paul instructed us to live in a way that is pleasing to the one who made the ultimate sacrifice. We are called to be instruments of righteousness (Romans 6:13), and it is this righteous living that eradicates the sinful life we once lived.

Jesus epitomized forgiveness with His death on the cross by taking upon Himself the sins of the world. The consequences, or wages of sin is death, but the Messiah grants us eternal life. As believers, there will be times in our lives that we will have to do things that seem unfair. Forgiving others may feel this way, but even when we have to make decisions that offend us, we delight in the fact that it pleases the Father.

When we forgive, it is similar to the death of Christ—grace that is unwarranted. We pardon despite feeling as if the transgressor does not deserve it. Extending compassion and mercy gives life to the one who is acquitted as well as the one who acquits. Jesus forgave at the cross, refusing to drink from the cup of bitterness, and was raised to life for all eternity. Our act of forgiveness enables a great exchange to take place in our hearts and minds. If we hold onto unforgiveness, we imprison the wrongdoing in our mind and ironically are held captive by our own thoughts. The offender is now controlling a part of our emotions. We can recognize this when we feel negative energy when this person is seen, spoken about, or thought of. If our mood can be changed by any of these occurrences, we may need to search our hearts for unforgiveness.

Unforgiveness also confines us to a stronghold of resentment and spite, which adversely affects how we treat others. We begin to search for faults, even when a particular shortcoming does not exist. We expect to be offended even if we are encountered by kindness. We become paranoid about vulnerability, so we put up walls to protect ourselves, not realizing our behavior prevents others from loving us for who we are. This is a miserable and self-mutilating way of life, which is quite the opposite of the freedom God affords us. Thankfully, God has given us directives in His word to properly guard our hearts.

Guard Your Heart

There is something very powerful that happens when we are offended by someone. This offense will either lead to a strengthening or a weakening of the heart, and everything we do and say exposes the condition of it.

"A good man brings good things out of the good stored up in him, and an evil man brings evil things out of the evil stored up in him. But I tell you that everyone will have to give account on the Day of Judgment for every empty word they have spoken. For by your words you will be acquitted, and by your words you will be condemned." -Matthew 12:35-37 (NIV)

This is not an admonition to put barriers and walls up to keep people from getting close to us, but it is a warning against allowing offenses to hurt us to the point that we hurt others. Luke 6:45 instructs us that the words that come out of our mouths will communicate the condition of our hearts. The ailment is usually fashioned by our environment, and even though we cannot control the behaviors of others, we can control how we respond. Retaliation is a natural response, and even the Old Testament law endorsed "an eye for an eye, and a tooth for a tooth (Exodus 21:24)," as due punishment for a criminal act. In Matthew 5, Jesus taught the opposite of this law by using a hyperbole. He imparted that if you are being sued for a shirt, to also give your cloak. The point He was making is to be more than willing to reconcile. When we do this, we exercise a love that covers a multitude of sin (1 Peter 4:8). Forgiving and accommodating for the sake of peace can leave us vulnerable, but it allows God to work in the midst of us. This does not mean that we will never feel insulted, but the way we respond to it reflects how well we have guarded our hearts.

When we get an injury to our physical body, we must clean it, cover it, and use antibacterial ointment in order for it to heal properly. For our emotional and spiritual wounds, God is our master physician. He not only heals our past hurts, but gives us His wisdom to assist us with present and impending offenses. He teaches us to surrender our concerns to Him because He is trustworthy to deal with it far better than we could without Him (1 Peter 5:6-7). We place our issues at His feet and relinquish the illusion of control, trusting that He will right the wrong.

To guard our heart, we must believe everything that God says about us, and negate everything the enemy would try to implant with the careless words and actions of others. The scriptures are filled with loving words from the Father that beautifully articulate how much we mean to Him. If we immerse ourselves in words of affirmation, it becomes easier to reject negativity. His Word is meant to encourage and empower us with the truth about our identity in Him. Anything that does not line up with the words God speaks over us is a repulsive lie. It may be easier for a wounded person to believe negative things about themselves because they are painfully aware of their perceived shortcomings. It is harder to believe in affirmations because we are not always aware of the greatness within us. We destroy negativity with positivity, trusting that we are made new in Christ.

"Therefore, if anyone is in Christ, he is a new creation. The old has passed away; behold, the new has come!" -2Corinthians 5:17 (ESV)

Our scars may reveal things we once did, but we are not our scars. They simply tell a beautiful story of a redemptive Father and His amazing grace. If we are new creatures in Christ, we do not behave in our old ways. There are new values and philosophies that we must adopt. These beliefs will form our new attitude that will reveal the God that lives inside of us. In addition to this indwelling, He gives us spiritual armor to help protect us from the enemy, and we must put this on daily.

Proverbs 4:23 reminds us to guard our heart. Those in Christ are presented with the armor of God. Each piece of the armor gives us protection for key components of our body that is vital for sustaining life. This armor is supernatural rather than physical. Because of the devious actions of others, it is easy to view people as our adversaries, but this is not so—they are merely the vehicle for the attack.

"For we do not wrestle against flesh and blood, but against the rulers, against the authorities, against the cosmic powers over this present darkness, against the spiritual forces of evil in the heavenly places."
-Ephesians 6:12 (ESV)

After we receive Christ as our personal LORD and Savior, it is the devil's personal enterprise to evoke and win every battle he wages against us. This is not to say that we should allow ourselves to be mistreated by others, but we must remember that it is unbecoming and inappropriate to avenge ourselves, even if we feel as if they deserve it.

The armor of God consists of the helmet of salvation, the breastplate of righteousness, the belt of truth, our feet readied with peace, the shield of faith, and the sword of the Spirit. Each piece of armor protects key components of our bodies, and the shield blocks what tries to find our vulnerabilities. Our weapon is the Bible, which is the infallible Word of God. The helmet protects the mind, and we must diligently put this on to defend ourselves from poisonous thoughts. The breastplate guards the heart, and we know that out of the abundance of the heart, the mouth speaks (Matthew 12:34). The belt of truth guards the waist. Since the belt is worn in the center of our bodies, the truth keeps us balanced. Peace guards our feet because no matter where we travel, we carry peace with us. In fact, as peacemakers (Matthew 5:9), we have the ability to change the atmosphere.

In combat, a shield is maneuvered to block attacks. Our prayers and knowledge of God's promises serve as our protection from the enemy's assaults. Lastly, our weapon is the Word of God. When we prepare for battle, we must grab our weapon. We cannot simply depend on what others say about God, we must know His word for ourselves and allow it revolutionize the way we think. If we sustain any damage, it has potential to adversely affect our heart. This will soon materialize in our actions, and these actions will impact those around us.

How do we combat offenses that were caused by others? First, we recognize that our real enemy is Satan. Satan understands that there is strength in numbers (Matthew 18:20), and will cause discord when there should be unity, so we must realize that he will work through people. He causes division by making us believe that humans should be at war with other humans, when in fact our battles are spiritual.

"For though we walk in the flesh, we are not waging war according to the flesh. For the weapons of our warfare are not of the flesh but have divine power to destroy strongholds." -2 Corinthians 10:3-4

Secondly, we put on the armor of God daily, and remind ourselves that we have every aspect of it. Third, we need to get rid of our pain. First Peter 5:6-7 (NLT) admonishes,

"So humble yourselves under the mighty power of God, and at the right time he will lift you up in honor. Give all your worries and cares to God, for he cares about you."

We can trust God to deliver us from the things we feel could destroy us. His power and might are more than enough to set us free from the bondage of hurt. He is capable of healing us instantaneously, but that does not mean we will never be tempted to go back to that place of sorrow. Satan will try to implant thoughts of defeat in our minds when we become overwhelmed by offenses. One of his tactics is infiltrated through time, reminding us of things that happened years ago. God is timeless and present in our now. With our willingness, God can take away the distresses we endure.

"Do not be anxious about anything, but in every situation, by prayer and petition, with thanksgiving, present your requests to God. And the peace of God, which transcends all understanding, will guard your hearts and your minds in Christ Jesus." -Philippians 4:6-7 (NIV)

Some may think of God as our resource only when problems are beyond our control, but this is not true. God desires intimacy with us and we can talk to Him the way we would talk to a human being about our issues. He desires to have a connection with us, and wants us to trust Him to set us free from strongholds. There is so much freedom when we allow the Father to work on our behalf. We may not always understand His plan, but there is great joy when the promise is fulfilled.

Our society makes it a point to say "get over it," without offering helpful resources to do so. This can be terribly difficult when we still have such painful memories, or may still be dealing with certain situations. To tell someone to 'get over it' implies that they must move on without properly dealing with their emotions. Eventually this will generate larger symptoms. Initially, this process may be painful, but the exchange for healing that takes place is worth more than gold. When we trust God and expose our wounds to the Savior, we throw them at His feet and leave them there. He is worthy of our trust in every area, and He desires to comfort us through our pain. The only way to get over a hurt is to give it to Jesus. Not only does our sanity and overall well-being depend upon it, but it dictates how we will interact with others.

If we love God then we will trust Him. When we trust God we learn how to love ourselves. When we love ourselves, we know how to truly love others. Loving others entails treating others the way we would like to be treated. When we love, we show that we belong to God and that He has dominion in our lives. This love includes walking in forgiveness. If we don't forgive, we don't love. If we don't love others, then we don't know God (1 John 4:7-8).

Jesus suffered greatly, and died so that we could be forgiven. In this life, we too, will be in a position where we must humble ourselves and forgive. Jesus displayed a love that led Him to have no regard for Himself. He yielded to the most brutal physical death to save us from eternal spiritual death. Because He forgives us we gain access to the Father. When we forgive others, they will see Jesus.

"For if you forgive other people when they sin against you, your heavenly Father will also forgive you. But if you do not forgive others their sins, your Father will not forgive your sins." -Matthew 6:14-15 (NIV)

According to Psalm 103, God throws our sins as far as the east is from the west. It would be highly hypocritical to know how badly we have sinned against God and hold grudges against others (Daniel 9:9). It is this standard of forgiveness that places a demand on the power of God. Without Him the result is discontentment and a lack of trust. Furthermore, the answers to our prayers are contingent upon our willingness to forgive. Forgiveness is an action that is connected to our prayers.

Reconciliation with God necessitates reconciliation with people. We cannot love God and hate people, despite how poorly they have treated us. In the body of Christ, we understand that we treat others the way that we would like to be treated (Matthew 7:12), even when we are not treated well. God cannot forgive us if we have not forgiven others. Matthew 5:23-24 tells us that if we have anything against another while making an offering to God, we must leave our gift at the altar, and go make things right with the person we have a conflict with. In this moment of reconciliation, our gift at the altar is humility.

Humility

First Peter 5:6-7 instructs us to humble ourselves before God, which requires us to be totally reliant on Him by abandoning our self-sufficiency. The scriptures teach us to let go of what we think is right and depend on the one who is. God speaks to us through His Holy Spirit who is our Guide and Advisor. The Counselor is committed to leading and instructing us in the way that we should go, but we must assume the responsibility to carry out the instructions.

Humbling ourselves may mean conducting an honest evaluation of our motives. It is a realization that we lack the power to fulfill the plan on our own. It is common for us to believe that we can carry our own burdens, but we serve a God who is not only willing, but able to exceed our greatest expectations (Ephesians 3:20). As we humble ourselves before Him, He bestows the divine exchange—our deficiency for His sovereignty.

"Come to me, all you who are weary and burdened, and I will give you rest. Take my yoke upon you and learn from me, for I am gentle and humble in heart, and you will find rest for your souls. For my yoke is easy and my burden is light." -Matthew 11:28-30 (NIV)

God is our strength, and it is in our weakness that He enables us to do what we are incapable of doing on our own (2 Corinthians 12:8-10). Humility is a vital component of forgiveness. There is nothing productive about holding unforgiveness in our hearts. It is a disease that spreads and causes bitterness, anger, rage, malice, and other ungodly characteristics. It is also true that spiritual maladies can affect physical conditions, so we must be on guard at all times.

When we humble ourselves, we show reverence to God. This places a demand on His power in the midst of our shortcomings. God is a Father who wants to provide for His children. This is not limited to physical provision since He is able to provide for every type of need we will ever have. Our meekness gives God the opportunity to demonstrate His authority. This dependency on God builds our trust in Him, which enhances our relationship with our heavenly Father (2 Corinthians 12:9-11).

Some may say that the key to be successful is to know and capitalize on strengths. In order to be a flourishing Christian, we must also know our weaknesses. If we do not, the enemy has a greater capacity to overpower us. Satan incessantly searches for our flaws, and orchestrates situations where they are revealed. That is why humility is vital. If we are not willing to allow God to operate in our weaknesses, we are willing to be defeated despite our strengths. The demise of Satan was concentrating on his strengths while disregarding his weaknesses. When he wars against us, he looks for the 'chinks' in our armor. He is seeking out the things that pester, frustrate, and throw us off of our game. This is what 1 Peter 5:8-9 is referring to. The best way to combat our enemy is to surrender to God (Isaiah 55:8-9), and depend on His power to bring us victory.

Humility in practice is awareness that we are intelligent beings, but if God is instructing us to do something different from what we have planned, we must trust that His way is far better. Humility is an invitation to allow the LORD to work on our behalf. When we are in tune with the Spirit of God, we give Him permission to lead us.

If we find that we are unsure of what He is saying, or we have no idea how to proceed, it is a good idea to take a time of consecration and fasting. Breaking away from the norm is a sacrifice of time and attention. The sacrifice can be food, television, social media, or anything else we can remove to make more time for God. This will prove to be an opportunity for spiritual growth. Fasting heightens our spiritual cognizance and responsiveness to the voice of God. We dedicate this time to the Father, putting Him before everything else. Our fasting signifies that He is more important to us than what we are sacrificing, and that He is worthy of such an offering. During this time God will show us what we need and how we can draw closer to Him. Even Jesus made this type of sacrifice in the wilderness, and as a reward for His obedience, He sits at the right hand of the Father.

Conflict Resolution

"If your brother or sister sins, go and point out their fault, just between the two of you. If they listen to you, you have won them over. But if they will not listen, take one or two others along, so that 'every matter may be established by the testimony of two or three witnesses.' If they still refuse to listen, tell it to the church; and if they refuse to listen even to the church, treat them as you would a pagan or a tax collector." -Matthew 18:15-17 (NIV)

One thing we must remember when it comes to confronting others is to discern how we respond to conflict. We must have a discussion with God before we talk to the offender, and certainly prior to consulting other parties. We need to take time to evaluate the situation and ourselves. Are we confronting this person because what they have done is wrong, or because we think we are right?

The purpose of the encounter should be to correct in love and reconcile our differences. If we see a brother or sister in Christ acting in ways that do not demonstrate holiness, then we are to make them aware of the situation in hopes that they will desire to change their behavior. However, it is not our responsibility to make them change;

it is only our responsibility to bring the need for change to their attention. In some circumstances, the person may not know that what they are doing is wrong. In other situations, they may be struggling with a particular sin and require assistance in that area.

The resolution should be to support them in averting the enemy, not to shame them. One of the most critical conditions of sin is self-deception. This disorder causes a person to believe that they are right when they are actually wrong. This can only be combatted with revelation knowledge that comes from God. Instead of trying to wear them down with the truth, this person must come into the knowledge of that truth for themselves, and then they will be set free (John 8:32).

Our prayers will greatly assist in this divine intervention. We cannot lose hope, even if it looks as if they will never change. We must realize that God gives all people the choice to choose Him, and the choice to choose the world. We may have seen these individuals lead powerful lives that influenced the Kingdom of God, and somehow they stumbled. Everyone has their own personal walk with God, and He, as the ultimate Judge, assesses in the end. We may want better for them, but they must want better for themselves.

After we have said what needs to be said, we prayerfully leave the rest to God. Prayer is one of the most powerful things we can do. When we pray it may seem as though things are getting worse, but prayer sends angels on the frontline to war on our behalf (Psalm 91:11). Our intercessions stand in the gap as we believe that we have overwhelming victory through Jesus Christ (Romans 8:37).

It is critical to discern that the verses in Matthew chapter 18 do not give us permission to be combative.

"Bear with each other and forgive one another if any of you has a grievance against someone. Forgive as the LORD forgave you."
-Colossians 3:13 (NIV)

People can be non-confrontational, argumentative, passive aggressive, or fall within any of these categories at different moments in time. Regardless of our style, we must be prayerful and tactful about the way that we approach situations of this nature. Most importantly, we must operate with humility, dutifully guarding our hearts against offense so that we do not become abusive with our words or actions. The goal of this meeting is to maintain peace and encourage those in the faith, so we cannot allow ourselves to become antagonistic. The other option is to not say anything at all, but if we are going to hide our contempt for the offender for the way we are being treated, we will be susceptible to sin, and these ill feelings will not produce holiness. This does not mean that silence is not an option, but we must take prayerful consideration in matters of this sort. It is vital that we guard our heart, especially when we are embarking upon this task. If we decide not to hold our brother or sister accountable, we must question our motives. We cannot be afraid of the outcome. If God has told us to confront them, then we should do so.

If we have brought the offense to the person privately, then among a few witnesses, and finally the church, and they still do not listen, Matthew 18:17 states that we should treat them as a pagan or a tax collector. This does not mean that we hate these people, and it may not involve severing ties, but it does indicate that the dynamics of that relationship must change. A typical relationship with a tax collector usually involves paying what is owed.

The thirteenth chapter of Romans discloses that we should give to those we owe, and we all owe each other love. Although the relationship has changed, we do not forsake our love for them. The time will come when the person will realize the error of their ways, and may desire to reconcile. When this happens, we welcome them back and praise God for the victory. When we 'bear with one another' we clothe ourselves with the fruit of the spirit. It is only by His Spirit that we are able to accomplish difficult things (Zechariah 4:6). Colossians 3:12 tells us to put on compassion, kindness, humility, gentleness, and patience. This verse gives the command to 'put on' these fruit of the Spirit. If we have to put them on, that implies that we do not innately possess these qualities.

It is important to be compassionate and try to understand the situation from their perspective. We don't necessarily have to agree with them, but we should try to understand as much as we are trying to be understood. Witnesses of an altercation can usually see from both perspectives and form conjectures from both sides. Such should be the case in a court trial. The judge or jury listens to both sides of the argument to make an informed decision. If we can all make a habit of stepping back to listen to what the other person is saying, we would have a lot less miscommunication.

James 1:19 instructs us to be quick to listen, slow to speak, and slow to become angry. This is putting humility and patience into practice. Sometimes how we say something can be far more damaging than what we say. In this case, we find that the most precarious part on the human body is the tongue.

"A gentle answer turns away wrath, but a harsh word stirs up anger."

-Proverbs 15:1 (NIV)

Controlling the tongue requires the power of the Holy Spirit, especially when we have been offended. The tongue is a very small member of the body, but can cause so much damage to both the listener and the speaker. James 3 reveals that the tongue holds a world of evil. It is like a small spark that can set an entire forest ablaze. The damage the tongue can cause is enormous, so it is important that we carefully apply the Word of God to our situations.

When we condition ourselves to ignore insults, we accept that we are only in control of ourselves. James 1:20 tells us that human anger cannot produce the righteousness of God. Human anger will lead us to saying or doing things we will regret later if we do not exercise restraint. It is better to take some time to allow God to heal us from what has happened rather than lashing out because we have been hurt. If we can bear with one another, and work through each other's differences, we have won a great victory for the Kingdom of God.

To have successful relationships there has to be communication, but we must remember the context in which the relationship functions. If an offense happens, it needs to be addressed so that resentment does not manifest. If we allow ourselves to be perpetually subjected to ill treatment without addressing the issue, or remove ourselves without any communication, it will only breed contempt, which will eventually surface in our words and actions.

Even Jesus called Judas out on his betrayal (Matthew 26:21). He did not love Judas any less, and it does not mean we love the people in our lives any less. The same concept is true about God. As our heavenly Father, He corrects us because He wants better for us, and we should want better for those we have relationships with. Continually burying our hurt feelings will result in an eventual explosion, or cause excruciating rifts that may destroy the relationship. If we are being led by the Spirit of God, we will operate in the fruit of the Spirit. Therefore, we trust and pray that the offender has an open heart about what we have to say, and is willing to reconcile.

It is not our responsibility to change people—that responsibility is left to God. Confronting in love enables us to guard our heart and grow spiritually and emotionally. It also improves our relationships with people because they become cognizant of the things we do and do not like. If they love us they will try their best not to offend anymore, but if we are offended, we should communicate with love, compassion, and forgiveness. Our purpose in addressing the issue is to express concerns that interfere with the relationship. It is best to be intentional and transparent about our expectations and desire to improve the connection.

As stated in Matthew 18, there are necessary steps to communicate if they are not receptive to our feedback. This may mean seeking counseling or giving the person some space, so we should be prayerful about our approach. Though we may expect a response after communicating our viewpoint, we must understand everyone's process time will vary. It is our hope that they would be responsive, but we cannot force them to give us an answer. If this occurs, we cannot attempt to control them with overly repetitive reminders, 'the silent treatment,' or other manipulative measures. These actions do not display the love of God.

Depending on the association we have with this person, we have to be open to the possibility that the situation may be left with non-closure. If this is the case, we should seek God regarding our next steps. None of us particularly enjoy being corrected, and most don't enjoy correcting, but if we care about the offender, we must bear with them in love and mercy. After we have done our part, we leave the rest to God, trusting that He has our best interest at heart, even if things do not end the way we would like them to.

Loving Like Jesus

"You have heard that it was said, 'Love your neighbor and hate your enemy.' But I tell you, love your enemies and pray for those who persecute you, that you may be children of your Father in heaven. He causes his sun to rise on the evil and the good, and sends rain on the righteous and the unrighteous. If you love those who love you, what reward will you get? Are not even the tax collectors doing that? And if you greet only your own people, what are you doing more than others? Do not even pagans do that? Be perfect, therefore, as your heavenly Father is perfect." ~Matthew 5:43-49 (NIV)

How we treat others is a direct reflection of how well we are guarding our hearts. It is difficult to treat someone kindly when they have behaved rudely, but there is a great reward when we counter cruelty with kindness. When we give to others with no expectation of compensation, God will bless us. In Matthew 5, it is recorded that Jesus said that God doesn't show favoritism, but all are graced with sun and rain. If the LORD doesn't show partiality, neither should we. In First Peter 1, the writer directed believers how to live among the ungodly. God does not take us out of our reality, but He places things inside of us that empower us to resist and overcome the world. We will still be faced with the challenges of life, but the difference is we refuse to respond the way the world does. Every piece of advice Peter offers places us in a state of discomfort. For example, 1 Peter 3:8-9 (NIV) states the following condition:

"Finally, all of you, be like-minded, be sympathetic, love one another, be compassionate and humble. Do not repay evil with evil or insult with insult. On the contrary, repay evil with blessing, because to this you were called so that you may inherit a blessing."

It is extremely challenging to be 'the bigger person.' Many of us have been in this predicament and have contended with God about our rights to be respected and how the treatment is unfair. If the other person is a believer, we may even add that this person is not behaving in a Christ-like manner. This reveals a sense of entitlement. God desires to deal with each individual, and there is something we can learn about ourselves even in unfair circumstances. We may want the other party to be dealt with, but God uses these predicaments to change what is in our own hearts.

While we may be looking to change others, He is looking to change us. We must look within ourselves before passing judgment on others, taking out our plank before we cast down their speck. Being humble makes us the bigger person because we are honoring that individual the way we would like to be honored. We may not realize it at the time, but this act of humility changes the atmosphere. What wrath we could have exhibited is dispelled by our compassion and gentleness. Initially, this may cause us to endure some suffering, as humility always does, but that suffering can never be compared to hearing, "Well done," coming from the lips of our Father (Matthew 25:21).

Now if we are children, then we are heirs—heirs of God and co-heirs with Christ, if indeed we share in his sufferings in order that we may also share in his glory. -Romans 8:17(NIV)

Unity

"And above all these put on love, which binds everything together in
perfect harmony." -Colossians 3:14 (ESV)

In Acts 10-11, a dramatic transformation occurred in
Simon Peter. Peter was a disciple of Jesus and an avid
commissioner of the Faith. However, he displayed some
discriminatory beliefs towards those who were not
circumcised (Galatians 2:11-14). Peter's discrimination was
due to a cultural worldview, and he believed he was correct
in his prejudice. As human beings, we will always have
differences that could potentially separate us, but what
connects us in the faith is our relationship with Christ.
Peter had an extraordinary experience with God, where a
vision of all kinds of beasts and animals were placed before
him and the voice of God told him to kill and eat. Because
of his Jewish culture, Peter knew that eating many of those
animals in the vision were prohibited, but God told him
not to call anything unclean that He has made clean. Soon
after, Peter has Gentile visitors invite him to their
commander's home. The Holy Spirit informs Peter that he
is to go with these men. Before his revelation from God, it
is quite possible that Peter would have declined this offer

because he believed that the faith should be shared with Jews before it was shared with Gentiles. In Acts 10:28-29, Peter's ideologies were changed by his encounter with God and because of his faith and obedience to the LORD, the commander's entire household was converted to Christ.

There are several very important things to note in these chapters. First, salvation is offered with equal opportunity to all. Anyone who believes in Him will not perish, but will have eternal life (John 3:16). In Acts 10:25-26, we see that Peter was held in high esteem, and to be in the presence of an Apostle must have been overwhelming for the centurion, so he bent down in veneration. Peter reminded the Roman officer that he was simply a man and should not be worshipped. No matter how highly esteemed we might be, God is the only one to be reverenced. We are only as good as God allows us to be, and it is all for the glory of His name (Romans 11:36).

Peter discovers that if God does not show favoritism, then neither should we. We may be more comfortable with those who have backgrounds similar to our own, but God loves us all, and we should desire for all to know Christ. In this revelation from God, Peter was told to kill and eat. Prior to this event, there were disagreements between the brothers ranging from food to circumcision. This dispute was due to the disparaging cultural differences of Jews and Gentiles. Peter's culture did not eat certain animals because of their custom. So Jews did not readily share a meal with those who did not follow their traditions. With this vision and Peter's humility, God tore down two institutions—one of the stomach, and one of the heart.

Upon receiving Christ, we are endowed with the Holy Spirit (Acts 11:16-17), and Peter realized that he should not deny this gift to anyone. In the text, Peter recalled the words that John spoke about water baptism. He said there would come a time where people would be baptized in the Holy Spirit. As Peter preached the Gospel, His Gentile audience received the Holy Spirit and spoke in other tongues. This was proof enough for Peter that God desired reconciliation for all.

Water baptism is still a critical component in professing our faith. The blood of Jesus Christ is the atonement for the stain of guilt on our lives. The righteousness of Christ redeems of us from the consequence of sin, cleansing us and making us worthy of His presence. This new life in Christ is a death to the life of our former selves. This new life joins us spiritually with other believers who also have this new life despite cultural, physical, or social differences. There is something very powerful and magnificent that comes from accepting other cultures and working together in unity. Galatians 3:28 (NIV) conveys,

"There is neither Jew nor Gentile, neither slave nor free, nor is there male and female, for you are all one in Christ Jesus."

Wonderful things happen when we share God's love with other ethnic and cultural backgrounds. God's love knows no boundaries, and when we put limits on who we demonstrate love to, we are exhibiting characteristics that do not belong to God. God is love, and His love produces unity.

Our love for others should demonstrate that Christ lives in us (John 14:19). In John 17:20-23, Jesus prayed for the body of Christ to have unity. He made a point to communicate that there is unity between the Father and the Son. Afterwards, He compares this oneness to the body of Christ. The body of Christ is one unit that operates by the power of the Holy Spirit. We can be sure that this union in Christ allows God's glory to manifest so that the world can come to know the Truth. In John 17:22, Jesus said that He has given us His glory so that we can become one.

Pastor Whitman Toland of Christ City Church in Greensboro has told the congregation that it takes a relationship with Jesus to stay in relationship with people.[6] There will be moments when people will do things that we do not agree with, or that irritate and frustrate us to the point where we want to disassociate ourselves from them. The power and grace of God allows us to stay together so that an unbelieving world can come to have faith in the one who called us to be united.

If we are going to be unified, we must have fellowship. When it comes to congregations, there are several options available. We can be in any part of the United States and see several different churches. Some are even within walking distances from each other. There is nothing immoral about this, for God has called many people to preach the Gospel, and we do not all learn the same way. However, there is irrefutable power when we join together as one.

"Make every effort to keep the unity of the Spirit through the bond of peace. There is one body and one Spirit, just as you were called to one hope when you were called;" -Ephesians 4:3-4 (NIV)

---

[6] Whitman, Toland. "The Wave of God" (Sermon, Sunday service, Greensboro, February 2, 2014).

Just as much as we should improve ourselves, we are meant to inspire and motivate others to do great things. This goes against the current social norm of hedonistic tendencies, where our own needs and wants surpass everything else. This should not be the case for those in the faith. Jesus made a reference that He and the Father are one, and that because we know Christ, we are also one with Him (John 17). If we are all called to be one in Christ, we should be united with one another.

When Jesus prayed that the body of Christ would have unity, it was so that the world would know Him. It is through Christ that we have unity, and it is by this unity in Christ that the world will see God. We cannot know God without first knowing Jesus, and if we love Jesus we will keep His commands. In John 17, Jesus gave the disciples the glory of God for the sake of unity. This glory can only come from God. It is a marvelous brilliance of radiant light that emanates His presence and His power. This power is the highest essence of God and speaks of His preeminence. This excellence resides inside of every believer, magnifying a Savior that we all desperately need. Because of Jesus, we are able to function on one accord. When believers are united in Christ, we manifest God's presence and authority. This oneness demonstrates what heaven looks like—people of all cultures forsaking their traditions to glorify the one and only true God. If we want to see more people saved for the Kingdom of God, we must intentionally unify with other believers.

This is not to say that there shouldn't be multiple churches. God calls all sorts of men and women to begin ministries. He does not want to dispel what makes us unique, but even our differences should point to the same cross. First Corinthians 12 teaches us about the various parts of a physical body working together for one common goal—the correct function of a human being. Paul tells us that the same is true for the body of Christ. All of the different gifts in the church are necessary for it to function properly. In verses 12-30, we find that each gift is significant, though people may hold some gifts in higher esteem than others.

If we all had the same part, we wouldn't be known as a body (v. 19-20). A body part has a specific task, but it cannot accomplish much else without other body parts, so they all work together for a common goal. Often, the jobs that are considered smaller or less desirable are normally not celebrated. These may be the members that clean the bathrooms, paint walls, fix doors, etc. Many times these things go unnoticed because they may not seem as illustrious as preaching, teaching, prayer, and prophecy.

In essence, those directing traffic in the parking lot should be celebrated just as the preacher is. In fact, our unpresentable parts, such as the work done behind the scenes, should be treated with special modesty. Parts that are seen are already honored, because we acknowledge the gift as we see it. In this passage, it says that God honors the hidden parts so that there is no division. We should all rejoice when one is commended. No matter how special we think one position is, honor should be given to everyone working for the Kingdom.

If one member of the team has suffered a loss, the entire team suffers a loss. If one member of the team is victorious, the entire team is victorious. Our response should be based on the notion that we operate with one mind under the authority of Christ. How do we continue to be united? We mourn when others suffer, and rejoice when others are celebrated. We operate in humility, acknowledging that Kingdom work can only be accomplished when we work together.

"He makes the whole body fit together perfectly. As each part does its own special work, it helps the other parts grow, so that the whole body is healthy and growing and full of love." -Ephesians 4:16 (NLT)

Our unity reflects our mindset, which should be in Christ. Though we are many different parts, we are one, and we function to reconcile a dying world to Christ. Believers in Christ are one unit. As one, we are the fullness of Him who fills everything in every way. What this means is that Jesus is the fulfillment of everything. He works in us and brings all things into completion for the glory of God. The crucifixion of Christ put to death every curse and every sin, and granted us eternal freedom from chains that bind us in darkness. It is only by His power and His might that we are saved and delivered. To know Jesus is to know God. Jesus would not have been successful if He had not been obedient to His Father. Because He did what the Father said, people were compelled to believe in Him. If we belong to God then the things that we do should bring glory to Him.

The truth of the matter is the world will hate us because of what we believe. This world belongs to Satan and he wars against believers. Even though we live in the world, the world does not live in us. We allow the Spirit of

God to renew our attitudes and change our old habits. This also includes prejudices and discriminatory actions. We love with the love of Christ to reconcile the world to the God who saves. We function in the knowledge and truth that is given to us by the Holy Spirit. We must strive for unity in the places God has called us, and serve with the gifts He has invested inside of us.

"So from now on we regard no one from a worldly point of view. Though we once regarded Christ in this way, we do so no longer. Therefore, if anyone is in Christ, the new creation has come: The old has gone, the new is here! All this is from God, who reconciled us to himself through Christ and gave us the ministry of reconciliation: that God was reconciling the world to himself in Christ, not counting people's sins against them. And he has committed to us the message of reconciliation. We are therefore Christ's ambassadors, as though God were making his appeal through us. We implore you on Christ's behalf: Be reconciled to God. God made him who had no sin to be sin for us, so that in him we might become the righteousness of God." -2 Corinthians 5:16-21 (NIV)

Greater Things

"Very truly I tell you, whoever believes in me will do the works I have been doing, and they will do even greater things than these, because I am going to the Father. And I will do whatever you ask in my name, so that the Father may be glorified in the Son. You may ask me for anything in my name, and I will do it." -John 14:12-13 (NIV)

Jesus sends us into the world to finish what He began by entrusting us with the Great Commission (Matthew 28:16-20). A life in Christ requires a life surrendered to God. The most terrifying part of surrender is when we immerse ourselves in the thoughts of uncertainty. As creatures of habit, the unknown can be frightening, but our faith in Christ will never put us to shame (Psalm 25:3).

Peter had an undeniable love for Jesus. In Matthew 14, the Bible records Jesus walking on water. It was dark and the waves were beating against the boat the disciples were in. Jesus walks towards them on the water, but they are afraid that He might actually be a ghost. Jesus comforts them, assuring them of who He is. In the midst of the disciples' terror, Peter asked to be able to walk on the water. Jesus obliges his request and Peter steps out of the boat and begins walking on water, just like Christ. Soon after, he becomes afraid because he saw strong winds and his fear caused him to sink. He cries out for Jesus to save him, and He does, but questions Peter about his doubt. When Jesus and Peter get inside of the boat, the winds stop and the disciples worship Him in reverence of His magnificent power.

When we are in the midst of turbulent times, and it seems as if we are alone, we can be sure that Jesus is with us. The disciples saw that He was coming towards them, but did not recognize Him for who He was. They had never seen Him walk on water, so they were not expecting Him in the way He presented Himself. In our own situations, God does not always show up and help the way we think that He should. At this moment in the text, Jesus did not stop the waves from crashing on the boat. Instead, He was with them and encouraged them not to be afraid. Peter took advantage of the opportunity to be close to the Savior. Instead of asking Jesus to come where he was, Peter requested to go out to Jesus.

We may not understand why we endure hardship, but seeking Christ is always the answer if we are going to overcome adversity. Jesus gave Peter the opportunity for his faith to grow by allowing him to walk on water. Peter could have asked Jesus for anything, but his desire was to be in His presence. Walking on water was a product of his faith, but even in his faith, he started to be persuaded by the things in his environment. The strong winds caused Peter to doubt, but you cannot see wind! Peter allowed fear to produce disaster that was not there. We cannot allow our minds to construct barriers that do not exist. Even in his doubt which caused him to sink, Peter believed that Jesus could save him, and He did. All who saw this event worshiped Jesus as the Son of God. The things we go through are a testimony to others. It allows the world to see God who loves and cares for us, and rescues us in our time of need.

What is the prerequisite to achieve greater things? John 6:28-29 (ESV) illuminates this for us:

"Then they said to him, "What must we do, to be doing the works of God?" Jesus answered them, "This is the work of God, that you believe in him whom he has sent."

Those of us who believe possess a fire within that cannot be contained. We are purified, willing vessels, powered by the Holy Spirit who lay down our lives for the sake of the cross. We are the body of Christ, ignited with passion, zeal, fellowship, and transformation. In our faith, we are equipped to encourage others. Our conversion gives us the means to change the world by advancing the Kingdom of God. Our 'greater' is the power of the Holy Spirit resonating inside of us. Everything that we do should bring glory to Christ, and because He is our mediator in heaven, He gives us access to heaven while we dwell on Earth. This access grants us authority to bind and curse in the mighty name of Jesus (Matthew 18:18)! When we are united with the mind of Christ, God allows us to do greater things than what Jesus did during His lifetime, because He has gone to the Father.

In our hope, we understand that our belief pulls on the power of Jesus Christ. If there is no need then no power is given, which is why Jesus tells us to ask in His name. If we do not ask, there is an implication that we are not in need. We must understand that we are always in need of His sovereignty. If we choose to operate in our own power, we are functioning at a subpar level, which results in very little evidence of Jesus Christ in our lives. In Him, we love with a love that is beyond ourselves. These experiences will challenge us, humble us, and express to the world that we rest and trust in a power that is mightier than our own. When we love, it should reflect the love that Jesus has for us. We forgive when it is undeserved, accommodate when we are inconvenienced, and serve when it is a disservice to do so. We love because we are loved, and forgive because we are forgiven.

In the body of Christ, we are many, but we are also one. The power of Christ works within us, enabling and strengthening us to do what could not be done apart from Him. We are not chosen because of what we do, we are chosen because of what we believe. It is by our belief that we receive His Spirit, and it is by His Spirit that we live. Because we are new creations in Christ, we are the resurrection—sinful creatures whose sinfulness was put to death, and raised to a life in Christ Jesus. It is only because of the righteousness accredited to us by our faith that we are made right with God. This does not suggest that we are flawless. Perfection will not come until the day of redemption. It does indicate that we are able to do things perfectly because we are connected to a power that never fails. In our weakness He makes us strong. Our humility draws us closer to the Father, and by His hands we receive the anointing to overcome all of our adversities.

Believers are called to be the fragrance and the aroma of Christ. This is similar to an aroma leading people to the table to eat. The fragrance builds suspense, tantalizes the senses, stimulates the mind, and produces eagerness. From the sense of smell, you can usually identify what is being prepared, but we never know how magnificent it tastes until we sit down at the table to eat. It is the same way with our lives. The things we say and do are the fragrance of who Christ is and what He has done for us. As the aroma of Christ, we should be drawing people to the table to eat with the Father. While Jesus offers salvation, we are His advocates, and our lives should spread the knowledge of who He is, attracting a starving world to the God who satisfies (2 Corinthians 2:14-16).

Jesus will do whatever we ask in His will if we do the works that He has done. Everything Jesus did is derived from one simple concept—Love God, and love others as we love ourselves. Our lives in Christ are not based on our capabilities, shortcomings, or feelings. Our hope and expectation are set upon the God who saves, and He gives us everything we need to accomplish His will. Because of Him, we will impact generations to come with the Gospel of Christ. In this life, we will face opposition, and trials will come, but overwhelming victory is ours through the power of Jesus Christ. As we exercise our faith, stand firm in our hope, and walk in love, we will do greater things.

"Peace I leave with you; my peace I give you. I do not give to you as the world gives. Do not let your hearts be troubled and do not be afraid."

-John 14:27 (NIV)

Bibliography

Strong, James. (2001). Anthistemi. *In The Strongest Strong's Exhaustive Concordance of the Bible.* Grand Rapids: Zondervan, 2001.

Strong, James. (2001). Katallage. *In The Strongest Strong's Exhaustive Concordance of the Bible.* Grand Rapids: Zondervan, 2001.

Strong, James. (2001). Krino. *In The Strongest Strong's Exhaustive Concordance of the Bible.* Grand Rapids: Zondervan, 2001.

Strong, James, *Meizon. In The Strongest Strong's Exhaustive Concordance of the Bible.* Grand Rapids: Zondervan, 2001.

Tenney, Merrill C. ed. *Zondervan's Pictorial Bible.* Grand Rapids: Zondervan, 1967.

Toland, Whitman. "The Wave of God." Sermon for Sunday service, Greensboro, February 2, 2014.

www.ingramcontent.com/pod-product-compliance
Lightning Source LLC
Chambersburg PA
CBHW060829050426
42453CB00008B/635